GREAT HOUSES OF WASHINGTON, D.C.

GREAT HOUSES
OF
WASHINGTON, D.C.

by HOPE RIDINGS MILLER

photography by CHARLES BAPTIE

conceived and produced by
WHITEHALL, HADLYME, & SMITH, INC.

Clarkson N. Potter, Inc./Publisher NEW YORK
DISTRIBUTED BY CROWN PUBLISHERS, INC.

CONTENTS

PREFACE

The Capital city has an extraordinary number of fine houses that are fascinating from the standpoint of exterior and interior design, and also because of their association with distinguished persons, past and present. Noted builders and wealthy owners were numerous in Washington, D.C., from the eighteenth century until after the Second World War, and foreign governments have built or bought several mansions in the city in the past half century.

"Great" as used in the title of this book follows *Webster*'s second meaning of the word: "Much higher in some quality or degree; much above the ordinary or average." Since this dual definition could apply to at least one hundred houses in Greater Washington today, the selection had to be limited. Thus, all residences included are within the District of Columbia; several "above average" houses in the metropolitan area, including nearby Maryland and Virginia, are omitted.

The White House and the President's guest house, Blair House, are omitted for two reasons: (1) Both are great houses of the United States, rather than of Washington proper; and (2) each is of such unimpeachable importance that neither could be treated comprehensively in a book that aims to spotlight other houses of distinction in the Capital city.

Magnificent embassy residences abound in Washington, but the eight featured here were selected because they were built to serve as homes for Americans, and were distinguished in Capital history before they became foreign properties. To a gratifying extent, in fact, development of the basic theme of the book has been an exercise in Americana; for, with one exception, each house mentioned in the book was designed by an American.

Since several of the structures date from the eighteenth or nineteenth century, history plays an important role in the book; and, in a number of instances, the emphasis has been on people—many prominent, some famous, in the earlier days of our country—rather than on architecture or interior design. Yet, all the distinguished historic dwellings in the city are not included, because even a cursory treatment of all would fill many books.

Georgetown, the oldest section of Washington, has many houses that are as extraordinary as the ones discussed here. Along Georgetown's N Street, alone, are several that are great, in the sense of both history and current interest. The Robert Todd Lincoln House (also known as the Laird-Dunlop House and the Laird House) at 3014 N Street, which dates from 1799, is exemplary of the proportion and refinement of the Federal period; it has had several notable owners, among them Robert Todd Lincoln. It is now the home of New Jersey's Representative Peter H. B. Frelinghuysen. Across the way, at 3017 N Street, is a brick dwelling that has been of particular interest in recent years. Once belonging to Newton D. Baker, Woodrow Wilson's Secretary of War, it was occupied by Mrs. John F. Kennedy just before she moved to New York, and later was the property of Michael W. Straight, author and editor. Mr. and Mrs. Noel J. Macy own the rose brick dwelling with classic white festoons on the façade at 3339 N Street. This house and the elegant one at 3337 N Street were part of "Cox's Row," six fine dwellings built about 1805 by Colonel John Cox, a prosperous merchant who later became mayor of Georgetown. Cox lived for a time at 3339, but he used the house next door for an elaborate party for Lafayette in 1824. Today, both are among the best examples of late Georgian architecture in Washington.

In other sections of the city there are still more houses that fit *Webster's* definition of "great," but any book has to stop—somewhere. So this one is an attempt to feature in detail, or briefly mention, thirty-four dwellings, dating from 1754 to 1967, that are *representative* of great houses of Washington.

For courtesies and assistance in assembling material, the author is indebted to: Mrs. Robert Low Bacon; Captain and Mrs. Peter Belin; Mrs. Patricia Firestone Chatham; Mrs. Fowler Wahl, social secretary of the Brazilian Embassy; Mme. Esenbel, wife of the Turkish Ambassador; Mrs. William P. Fay, wife of the Irish Ambassador; John Greer; Lady Lewis; Mr. and Mrs. John A. Logan; Mme. Lucet, wife of the French Ambassador; Señora de Margáin, wife of the Mexican Ambassador; the Marquesa de Merry del Val, wife of the Spanish Ambassador; Mrs. George Maurice Morris; Mrs. Claiborne Pell; Armistead Peter, III; Marvin C. Ross, Curator of Hillwood; the Belgian Ambassador, Baron Luis Scheyven; Miss Sue Shivvers, Washingtoniana Division, Washington Public Library; George Williams; Miss Mathilde Williams, Curator of the Peabody Room, George-town Library; and the staff of the Rare Book Room, Library of Congress.

H. R. M.

GREAT HOUSES OF WASHINGTON, D.C.

I

THE LINDENS

One of the finest examples of Georgian architecture in this country, and the most unusual of the great houses in Washington, is The Lindens, the home of Mrs. George Maurice Morris at 2401 Kalorama Road.

The house was built in Massachusetts almost twenty years before a doughty band of revolutionaries, disguised as Indians, staged the historic Tea Party in Boston Harbor. Today, hundreds of miles from its original location, it is a mid-eighteenth-century masterpiece, which was transported to, and restored in, the nation's Capital in the 1930's.

The story actually begins when Mrs. Morris as Miriam Hubbard was growing up in Chestertown, Maryland, in a house built in 1760. Keenly interested in history at an early age, she was particularly fascinated by antiques. As a young matron, she started collecting Queen Anne and Chippendale pieces, with the hope of one day owning an old house that would be a suitable setting for them.

Her husband, who was to become a distinguished lawyer and president of the American Bar Association, shared her interest, and encouraged her aim. Her devotion to the eighteenth century finally focused her attention on Westover, the classic mansion built in Charles County, Virginia, by William Byrd II. Mrs. Morris particularly liked the exterior of Westover and considered the possibility of duplicating it in Washington with the kind of mid-Georgian interior she had long visualized.

She had just purchased an eighteenth-century room from a Sussex County, Virginia, house (circa 1765) when the stock-market crash of 1929 shattered prospects for carrying out her plan. She gave the Virginia room to the Smithsonian Institution, but she still cherished the hope of one day owning an eighteenth-century house.

A friend suggested that she might find one somewhere and have it moved to Washington with less expense than would be required to duplicate the exterior of Westover. The idea appealed to her. After all, she reasoned, even a replica of Westover would be just that—a copy of the real thing. An extraordinary old house that could be restored to its original beauty would be preferable. She decided to look for one.

Approach to The Lindens from the sidewalk.

Her collection of Chippendale and Queen Anne sofas, wing chairs, highboys, and serving tables was waiting, and so was a sizable lot which she and her husband had purchased on Kalorama Road.

The setting had been carefully chosen. The broad, quiet street in one of the city's most exclusive residential areas takes its name from the historic tract that describes a wide horseshoe curve west of Connecticut Avenue, between Florida Avenue and Rock Creek Park. The section is something of a memorial to Joel Barlow, the noted diplomat and poet. He purchased several hundred acres from the Holmead family in 1807 and had the manor house at S Street and Phelps Place remodeled under Benjamin Latrobe's supervision, calling it Kalorama, the Greek equivalent of "beautiful view."

Distinguished citizens have long been attracted to the section. Five Presidents, before or after terms in the White House, have lived there: Woodrow Wilson, for three years before his death, at 2340 S Street; William Howard Taft, as Chief Justice (1921–1930), at 2215 Wyoming Avenue; Warren G. Harding, as a senator from Ohio (1915–1921), at 2314 Wyoming Avenue; Franklin D. Roosevelt, as Assistant Secretary of the Navy (1913–1921), at 2131 R Street. Charles Evans Hughes as Chief Justice lived at 2223 R Street, and his successor, Harlan Fiske Stone, lived at 2340 Wyoming Avenue. Senator J. William Fulbright has resided at 2527 Belmont Road for a number of years, and Robert S. McNamara, former Defense Secretary, then president of the International Bank for Reconstruction and Development, lived at 2412 Tracy Place. The area also has its share of foreign embassy residences.

With the hope of finding an old house that would do honor to the distinguished community and, most of all, meet certain personal requirements, Mrs. Morris began a protracted search that took her from South Carolina to Maine. The "personal requirements" were that the house should be (1) mid-Georgian or earlier—that is, built between 1700 and 1790; (2) adaptable to modern living; (3) truly distinctive in at least one feature; and (4) destined for demolition unless purchased and moved.

In Danvers, Massachusetts, Mrs. Morris found a dwelling that met all the requirements—and more. The largest wooden house ever constructed in the Colonies, it was on the verge of being stripped and possibly destroyed. The elegant, uncluttered exterior, the singularly attractive hallway, and the gracious proportions inside and out offered the kind of restoration possibilities that Mrs. Morris was seeking.

Others had already noted the basic beauty of the house and ascertained the value of its fine woodwork. Antique dealers were bidding for its components by lots, and the original drawing room with its New England colonial panelings and Corinthian pilasters had been purchased by the William Rockhill Nelson Gallery and Atkins Museum of Fine Arts in Kansas City, Missouri.

The house had an interesting history. It was built in 1754 by Robert Hooper, an ardent Tory and a Marblehead merchant prince, whose wealth and flair for luxurious living prompted acquaintances to call him "King" Hooper. The sobriquet was especially apropos after Hooper ordered a stately

Entrance hall.

Central staircase.

coach, a copy of one belonging to King George III, to carry him regularly from Marblehead to Boston. With a majestic gesture, he removed the first obstacle to his regal itinerary—a corner house around which his outsized conveyance could not pass. He simply purchased the dwelling and had a broad passageway cut through to accommodate his coach.

Fittingly enough, Hooper's grand new home was called The Great House, a name that continued through pre-Revolutionary days. Later, as summer headquarters for British General George Gage, it was known as Gage House, and then, for a time, as "The House of the Front Door with the Bullet Hole." The story is told that as General Gage was entering the house one morning, a colonial soldier took a shot at him—and missed. The bullet made a large hole in the front door. It is still there.

Early in the twentieth century, the house came to be called The Lindens, because of the trees surrounding it. The purchase of the property by Mrs. Morris was completed in September, 1934, and arrangements were promptly made to dismantle—in fact, dismember—the structure for shipment to Washington. Over a period of seven diligent weeks, the house was taken apart and the pieces carefully numbered to correspond to a master plan before being loaded onto six freight cars. The remarkable move was accomplished with incredibly few mishaps. Except for a scratched doorstep, some cracked windowpanes, and a slightly damaged dormer sash, the entire shipment arrived in Washington intact, down to the handmade nails and the front door with the bullet hole.

Two years and nine months went into the reassemblage under the supervision of Walter Mayo Macomber, former resident architect of Colonial Williamsburg and now resident architect of Mount Vernon and Stratford, the birthplace of Robert E. Lee.

The Lindens, restored, was cited in *Antiques* magazine as "one of America's fairest colonial mansions." It is that, indeed; it is also distinguished on many other accounts.

In the best Georgian tradition, the exterior symbolizes masculine simplicity and quiet dignity. Three sides are clapboarded, but the rusticated sandstoning of the entrance façade contrasts nicely with the lighter angle quoins, window lintels, and doorway frame, giving the whole a classic dignity that is accentuated by the splendid central pediment and columns with handsomely carved Corinthian capitals. Grace of form and detail are also emphasized in the gambrel roof with the balustraded deck at the ridge, the asymmetrical chimneys, and the alternating angular and semicircular gables of the dormers.

An especially impressive memento of the Georgian period, one which does much to make the interior of The Lindens one of the most beautiful in the United States, is the high-ceilinged entrance hall, twelve feet wide and forty-two feet long. In spacious contrast to many cramped colonial halls with their steep, narrow stairways, it has a handsome spiral staircase, with gracefully turned balusters and finely molded steps, all typical of intricate Queen Anne workmanship at its best.

The outstanding attraction of the hall, however, is the scenic wallpaper,

Dufour's wallpaper in the entrance hall.

11

printed in France, in shades of blue, vermilion, gray, and green. The mural effect depicts Dufour's "Voyage d'Anténor" (c. 1814) and "Télémaque dans l'île de Calypso" (c. 1825), and "Les Incas," inspired by Marmontel's eighteenth-century novel and printed by Dufour's successor, A. Leroy, in 1832. Experts say that The Lindens is the only house in the world with three complete sets of French nineteenth-century hand-blocked wallpaper.

A member of the Peabody family of Massachusetts who owned The Lindens for many years acquired the wallpaper from a factory in Mulhouse, Alsace. Although the oldest of the sets is seventy years younger than the house, all three are so completely harmonious with the setting that Mrs. Morris could not resist having them moved and rehung.

The transposition posed quite a problem, however. The wallpaper had to be steamed off in wide strips with painstaking care, and each piece had to be reinforced with linen backing before being turned over to an artist for restoration. But when the process was completed, the wallpaper was once more in perfect condition, the scenes as clear and lovely as they probably were when first hung more than a century ago.

Even more unusual than the wallpaper are the elaborately decorated floors in the hall and several of the rooms. Achieved by stenciling center-pieces and borders of fruit, leafage, and scrolls on the wide pine boards, the designs are reputed to be the oldest known examples of this treatment in America, and are beautiful reminders of an art that first flourished in England as early as 1739.

The house is markedly enhanced by the furniture collection, which was acquired by Mrs. Morris over a period of forty years. Each carefully selected piece is an original, in keeping with the character of the house. Drapery designs throughout follow those pictured and described in Chippendale's *Gentleman and Cabinet-Maker's Directory*, published the year the house was built, and all the materials have been chosen to correspond to the era. Not a curtain or valance is of later date than 1754.

Drawing room.

The drawing room today is a faithful reproduction of the original, now in the William Rockhill Nelson Gallery. The walls are painted a delicate gray-green. Curtains in gold brocatelle hang from Chippendale cornices covered with matching material.

Pilasters on plinths decorate both sides of the fireplace, which, simplicity itself, has no mantelshelf. Paneled doors near the fireplace open to the chimney closets.

Most of the furniture is from New England and Pennsylvania. Over the eighteenth-century Philadelphia tables on either side of the door to the hallway are English candle brackets, which have prisms festooning their glass arms. The Philadelphia Chippendale sofa has been cited as one of the finest of its kind. It has gracefully molded legs, a slightly curved seat, and points flanking the arched back. Other extraordinary pieces in the room are: a Marlborough footed wing chair; a pedimented secretary; a handsome oriental carpet, typical of those used in many notable American homes of the eighteenth century; a cupboard with gently curved shelves (called "butterfly shelves") and original marbleizing; and a display of 1750–1760 China Export

armorial porcelain, which Mrs. Morris found in London, and which bears the motto and coat of arms of the Ross family, to which her late mother belonged.

More of this porcelain appears in the dining room, in a shelled cupboard with a Chinese lacquer red background, which blends with the eighteenth-century red damask curtains. The woodwork here is in the original blue shade. The dining table is a three-part tripod of the type that was highly popular in the late 1700's. The twelve New York Chippendale chairs once belonged to the Revolutionary General Matthew Clarkson, whose daughter married the son of John Jay, first Chief Justice of the United States.

Mahogany serving tables, three Georgian gilt mirrors, and four antique silver candle brackets with hurricane globe shades are other items that attract special attention in the dining room.

Upstairs, one of the inviting guest chambers has gray woodwork warmed with peach-colored walls, a corniced Chippendale bed draped with crimson damask to match the window hangings, an unusually handsome mahogany chest-on-chest, made in Philadelphia, and a great wing chair.

Charles II crewelwork (worsted embroidery on a cloth background), curtaining the windows and draping the canopied Queen Anne bed, is notable in Mrs. Morris' own bedroom. A William and Mary highboy with trumpet-turned legs also enhances this chamber, which Helen Comstock acclaimed in her book, *The 100 Most Beautiful Rooms in America*. (Also pictured in the book is the main hallway of the house.)

Another bedroom, called the "green room," has blue-green woodwork and pale yellow walls. It contains a Chippendale bed simply draped in printed cotton with bold figures and bright colors, a prim claw-and-ball foot New England desk with Chippendale mirror above, a harmonizing chest, and three Queen Anne chairs.

In the pink bedroom, a Chippendale bed with slender posts made in Salem is draped with toile de Jouy bearing the stamp of S. S. Oberkampf et Companie. A Chippendale chest and a Queen Anne highboy are other notable antiques here.

The Lindens is a far cry from the English stereotype of an eighteenth-century American home as a primitive log cabin, constantly threatened by Indians; and yet the original architect-carpenter either took into account the possibility of an occasional redskin raid, or wished to provide "King" Hooper with a means of quick access to his wine cellar. In any event, incorporated into a panel of the drawing room is a secret door, operated by a concealed spring and opening into a passageway to the library, and leading by a steep, narrow stairway to the cellar.

The recreation room in the basement is decorated in the tradition of an old tavern dance hall. The walls are part plastered and part finished with old pine sheathing. There are two big fireplaces, and the room can be divided by unhooking and dropping a panel partition that is hinged to a central ceiling beam.

The dining room, centered with a three-part tripod table and New York Chippendale chairs.

Master bedroom, featuring Charles II crewelwork.

The long trestle table is made of maple with a pine top, reputed to have been found in Cherry Valley, New York, about the time of the massacre there. Mrs. Morris believes it may have antedated the massacre by many years; but, anyway, it serves admirably at her eighteenth-century soirees featuring Fish House punch and other eighteenth-century specialties.

Mrs. Morris is a dedicated antiquarian—but a practical one. Her determination to make her restored mansion authentically beautiful did not prohibit her from including twentieth-century conveniences. She was delighted, however, when her exhaustive research turned up some interesting oddments, indicating that workable precursors of modern appurtenances for comfort appeared in select homes centuries ago. She learned that privileged persons in the Aegean civilization had baths as far back as 1700 B.C.; that semilegendary King Minos, who reigned over Crete three generations before the Trojan War, had a flush toilet in his palace; and that colonial Americans of wealth sometimes ordered shower baths from London.

The Lindens has six bathrooms, a modern kitchen, and central heating; however, most of the modern appointments are either closed off or cleverly disguised. The piano in the recreation room stands behind a panel. Telephones are concealed in antique cabinets. The television receiver in Mrs. Morris' bedroom is on a table that can be rolled into a closet at a moment's notice. Dummy book panels hide the radio in the library, where the only modern electric lamps are also unobtrusively located. The remainder of the house is lighted by electric candles in genuine wax casings.

Recreation room viewed from the big fireplace at one end.

Early American enthusiasts sometimes are surprised to find venetian blinds at The Lindens, but Mrs. Morris can cite eighteenth-century approval of their use in a 1762 advertisement of a Boston firm, which proclaimed them "the greatest invention ever made by man."

Mrs. Morris' meticulous attention to detail, in fact, is largely responsible for the overall excellence and validity of the restored mansion. An inveterate researcher, she tracked down answers to innumerable, seemingly unimportant questions that arose before the work was completed, and became an expert on houses and furnishings—and also manners and customs —of the eighteenth century.

For example, she spent months trying to find out how servants were summoned. Were they called by bells manipulated by pulls? If so, what kind? She queried several authorities in America, and then the Victoria and Albert Museum in London. When no answers were forthcoming, she began exhaustive research on her own, and finally discovered that bell pulls were, indeed, used in the eighteenth century in England and America, and that a London antique shop could supply her with needlework examples.

Since its completion in November, 1937, The Lindens has welcomed some forty thousand visitors, including many from foreign lands, and it has won authoritative acclaim from many sources. In his excellent book *Early American Architecture*, Hugh Morrison pays especially fitting tribute to the house as a whole and to its rooms, "which combine richness with restraint, which merge sophistication with fine simplicity, and . . . perfectly balance beautifully calculated surfaces with the volumes of space they compose."

The library.

16

II

HILLWOOD

For sheer magnificence of vistas and gardens and interior furnishings of museum value, no other house in Washington rivals Hillwood, the Linnean Avenue home of Mrs. Merriweather Post.

In a class by itself, the Georgian dwelling sits in majestic possession of many treasures unique in America, dominates a twenty-four-acre estate on the edge of Rock Creek Park, and commands a spectacular view, including the Washington Monument more than six miles away.

The owner's flair as a collector is reflected in the decorative arts from eighteenth-century France and Imperial Russia that accent the interior. Each room has its own cachet of surprise and elegance; each is a complete picture within itself and yet an integral contributor to a house that revives Old World grandeur in an efficient twentieth-century setting.

Mrs. Post's concentration on two fascinating cultures, and her taste in selecting and displaying her diverse assemblage has given it a cohesive quality. French eighteenth-century masterpieces and Russian Imperial art treasures, often side by side, emphasize her dichotomy of interests as a collector and also serve as visual reminders of the French influence on artists and craftsmen who furnished palaces for the czars.

Mrs. Post's devotion to the French eighteenth-century period preceded by a number of years her interest in the art of Imperial Russia. The latter engaged her from the time she acquired an exquisite Fabergé snuffbox from the Yussupoff collection in 1927, and noted the similarity between this little masterpiece of amethyst quarters, rubies, emeralds, and diamonds made in Saint Petersburg, and French eighteenth-century objects of art.

She began collecting other Russian effects, in earnest—icons, chalices, porcelain, and tapestries from 1936 to 1938, when she was the wife of Joseph E. Davies, the United States Ambassador to the Soviet Union. Visiting warehouses filled with Imperial Russian memorabilia offered for sale to embassy personnel, she found and purchased many dust-covered and tarnished objects that recalled long-forgotten chapters of Russian history.

Hillwood, which Mrs. Post acquired in 1955, was one of many mansions to be tailored specifically to both her extraordinary treasure trove and her

Hillwood, from the garden terrace.

gracious way of life. She spent two years redesigning the house and transforming the grounds into a fabulous complex of gardens on a truly grand scale.

The house was originally built in 1926 by John Diebert for Colonel and Mrs. Henry Parsons Erwin. They had the red brick structure designed so that the axis of the house would afford a view of the Washington Monument in the far distance, above the lush valley of Rock Creek Park.

Typically late Georgian, the house was styled with a flat roof, rimmed with a balustrade. The English atmosphere was emphasized in the interior with Jacobean furniture and Tudor paneling in the large library that had two mantels and extended across most of the terrace side of the house.

The grounds were planned for the enjoyment of a family of five. The Erwins liked to ride horseback, and there was an ample stable. They liked to swim, and a swimming pool was a center of interest on the lower terrace. They liked flowers, and there were rose gardens and a greenhouse. There was also a picturesque *allée*, bordered with English box, from the portico to the lower terrace.

Not long after Colonel Erwin's death, Mrs. Post purchased the estate and initiated many changes. She had the roof raised, and added dormer windows. Trees that obstructed the view of the Washington Monument were cut down by the dozens so that the pristine shaft could be clearly seen from the house. Underbrush was cleared from the grounds, and planting on a thoroughly organized basis was begun.

Meanwhile, the house itself underwent further dramatic transformation. The dining room was enlarged, and a bay was added to accommodate a breakfast room looking out onto the terrace. What had been the Erwins' enormous library became several rooms: a smaller library, part of a French salon, and special rooms for Mrs. Post's priceless icon and procelain collections. A spacious pavilion, designed as a little theatre and picture gallery, was added to the north front.

There were innumerable other changes, including the name of the estate. Colonel and Mrs. Erwin had called it Abremont ("wooded arbor"); Mrs. Post renamed it Hillwood.

Regarded as the most complete estate within the bounds of Washington today, Hillwood, in the words of a person who visits it often, "has everything except a shopping center."

It was rated Number One, according to the 1961 listing of Washington's ten costliest homes on the basis of tax assessments. The report also pointed out that in addition to the main house with its thirty-six rooms and six baths Hillwood includes a brick chauffeur's house and garage; a six-room, three-bath, air-conditioned steward's house; a brick butler's house; a twelve-room, three-bath staff's quarters; a seven-room gardener's cottage; a brick garage and stable; two greenhouses; and a gatehouse.

The splendor of the estate is symbolized by the main entrance gate, with its original posts and early Georgian grilles that were cast in 1736 for Halstead Place, Kent, England. Surmounting the posts are carved porthcawl stone urns, originally designed for the Paulston-Ringwood estate in Hamp-

Porte cochere and forecourt centered by statue of Eros.

Formal French garden.

21

shire, England; and flanking the gates are handsome English lampposts that were restored after being bombed in World War II.

Proceeding up the winding driveway in autumn or spring, one sees a riot of blossoming color and a profusion of verdant loveliness. All the varieties of trees that can thrive in the Washington climate are represented at Hillwood, and each has been placed with studious regard to color, texture, and surroundings. Plants include more than four thousand azaleas, hybrid rhododendron, dogwood, flowering cherry and crabapple trees, Japanese, Chinese, English, and American holly trees, ten varieties of snapdragons, and thousands of tulips and roses.

There are gardens within gardens, complemented with fine statuary and manicured shrubs that give the grounds the effect of a royal park. There are cutting gardens, a garden terrace, a tulip and rose garden, and a formal French garden just off the Louis XVI drawing room.

The Japanese garden on the lower terrace is an oriental dream of arched moon bridges, stone carvings artfully arranged among flowers and shrubbery, temple lanterns, mountains, and a miniature lake, a waterfall, a statue of Buddha, and stone lions on guard at the entrance.

Nearby, a pixie terrace is the setting for four fairy-like figures playing musical instruments, and not far away a secluded dog cemetery is surrounded by a low cast-iron fence, landscaped with weeping dogwood, and planted with dogtooth violets, forget-me-nots, bleeding hearts, and pansies.

Near the dog cemetery is the newest stellar attraction on the estate. It is a picturesque Russian *dacha,* built to house the collection of Russian art objects, which were given to Mrs. Post by Signora Rosso. The latter is the widow of Augusto Rosso, who was Italian Ambassador in Moscow when Mrs. Post was the wife of the then United States Ambassador to the Soviet Union, Joseph E. Davies.

Reached through the rose and tulip garden on the upper terrace is "Friendship Walk," overlooking the city and the lower gardens. Envisioned and promoted by George Livingston Williams, author of *The Gardens of Hillwood,* Friendship Walk was a gift to Mrs. Post from 113 friends who presented it to her in November, 1957. (Almost a decade later—in March, 1967—many of these friends and others feted Mrs. Post at a reception at the Sulgrave Club. The occasion was her eightieth birthday, and the gift presented to her was a pair of Imperial Russian candelabra in lapis lazuli with ormolu, which now flank a matching vase in the icon room of Hillwood. To the contributed funds left over after the gift was presented, Mrs. Post supplied the amount necessary to buy a masterwork which was commissioned by Catherine the Great in memory of Potemkin in 1791.

The front entrance of Hillwood with its porte cochere and neatly clipped hedges has a driveway circling a grass plot, bordered with swags of ivy and centered with a marble statue of Eros, reaching back with one hand to draw an arrow, and shielding a kid with the other. Predating 1830, this interpretation of the God of Love, which once graced Princess Faucigny Lucinge's Château Vaux le Penil, is an engaging herald of the Old World treasures that are beautifully displayed within the house.

Japanese garden.

The extraordinary spectacle is apparent from the moment one steps into the central hallway. There are feasts for the eyes in every direction, including a Louis XVI marble table bearing a bust of the Duchess of Chateauroux, one of the mistresses of Louis XV; and over the stairway there is a royal Russian portrait gallery with paintings of Catherine the Great, Grand Duke Paul, Alexander II, Alexandra Feodorovna, the last czarina, and a marble medallion of Nicholas II, the last czar.

The magnificent rock-crystal chandelier is from the palace of Paul I at Gatchina near Saint Petersburg. Imperial Russian vases adorn French eighteenth-century commodes, and a Louis XV jewel cabinet, decorated with dolphins, contains an original grant of title from Czarina Elizabeth in 1743.

From the center of the hallway, as one looks directly ahead, the Washington Monument is impressively visible. To the left of the hallway, lighted wall cabinets in the foyer off the dining room display exquisite Sèvres porcelain; one tureen was designed by Duplessis in 1754 and ordered by Madame de Pompadour. To the right is the Russian porcelain room, with the French drawing room beyond it.

Containing the finest collection of its kind outside Russia, the twelve-sided porcelain room is lined with lighted cabinets showing the four services ordered by Catherine the Great for use when she dined annually with knights of her four imperial orders; also here is a collection of imperial stars, badges, ribbons, and rare glass goblets, as well as a tumbler etched with the Russian Imperial eagle and dated 1747.

Equally fascinating is the icon room with a monumental array that is unique in this country: chalices and elaborate chalice covers, a rare tapestry rug on the wall and one on the floor showing the Orlov coat of arms, a large cabinet in ebony, ormolu, and lapis lazuli, a collection of Russian silver and enamel objects, and a silver gilt incense burner made in Moscow in 1691.

In a circular showcase are creations of Peter Carl Fabergé, the goldsmith and court jeweler, whose original establishment in Saint Petersburg reached preeminence during the reigns of Alexander III and Nicholas II. Two of Fabergé's Imperial Easter eggs are shown: the monogrammed egg in royal blue enamel, which Alexander III ordered for his wife, and the celebrated pink egg, which Nicholas II gave to his mother in 1914. Of special interest, also, is the elaborate little Fabergé snuffbox that stimulated Mrs. Post's interest in Russian Imperial decorative art in 1927.

Another museum within itself is the Louis XVI drawing room, with its fine wood paneling from a château near Paris, a white marble mantel decorated with ormolu from a French palace, and tapestries woven at Beauvais after cartoons by Boucher. Winterhalter's 1857 portrait of the Empress Eugénie hangs over the mantel, and cabinets on either side feature Sèvres porcelain—*bleu céleste* and *rose Pompadour.*

On the wall opposite the fireplace, a portrait of Louise Elizabeth de France hangs above an ornate desk, which is adorned with the cipher M A (for Marie Antoinette) and decorative motifs symbolizing the arts and sciences. Two sofas and twelve chairs with tapestries commissioned by Louis XVI and Marie Antoinette for a gift to Prince Henry of Prussia are further features of this salon, along with a pair of sofas and four chairs in gilt by

Main hallway.

A corner of the icon room.

The porcelain room,
with a glimpse of the
drawing room.

Georges Jacob, a collection of rare West European goldsmith's works and watches, and a large Savonnerie rug, woven about a century ago.

English effects are combined with French and Russian in the library. Most of the furniture is English, including Queen Anne armchairs, Sheraton and Regency commodes, and a William and Mary walnut circular stretcher table. The Georgian paneling was carved from pine. Above the Adam-style mantelpiece, which also came from England, is Sir Oswald Birley's portrait of Mrs. Post's father, Charles Williams Post, who founded the Postum Cereal Company. Across the room, a portrait of her mother is framed in limewood, carved by Grinling Gibbons.

The ornate coffee table in front of the large sofa was made in Moscow in the eighteenth century. The smaller table with a malachite top is also Russian. Russian papier-mâché boxes, and a rare collection of Flemish and German tankards in ivory mounted in silver attract special attention here, as do the paintings, which include a portrait of Mrs. Post by Frank Salisbury.

Missing in the room is a painting of the historic ship, the *Constitution*, done by J. C. Evans in 1837 and given by Mrs. Post to the Museum of the U.S. Naval Academy not long ago. Originally, she acquired the picture to hang in the *Sea Cloud*, the finest of the yachts she has owned. (The *Sea Cloud* is featured in a series of framed photographs that decorate the walls of the cozy telphone room just off the transverse hallway near the main entrance.)

In the corridor from the library to the dining room, there are displays from the Imperial Porcelain Factory, colored biscuit figurines, Russian portraits and landscapes, and watercolors and prints illustrating events in Russia of the last century.

Another fascinating passageway leading to the pavilion exhibits a wide variety of rare minerals, lavender, tinted jade, pieces of Sèvres services, and a big palace vase made in the Imperial Porcelain Factory about 1860.

The pavilion is a charming room of no particular period, with walls swagged in orchid velvet and draperies of royal purple, an inlaid Adam floor, and lighted cases filled with Imperial porcelain and palace vases. There are portraits of Czar Alexander I and Catherine the Great, Emperor Franz Joseph and Empress Elizabeth; also portraits of Mrs. Post and her daughters from 1918 until 1938, when she was presented at the Court of St. James's.

Lighted by magnificent twin chandeliers, the dining room is one of the more regal areas of the house. The French Regency paneling came from an old house in Paris, and four colorful hunting scenes were painted about 1775 by the famed Dutch master, Dirk Langendyk.

Virtually every effect in the room has a fascinating story. The beautiful Aubusson rug, which remained in storage for seventy-five years before being brought to this country, was ordered as a gift from the French court to Emperor Maximilian and Empress Carlotta of Mexico. The French empire sideboard with Sèvres plaques and bronzes by Thomire was given by the French people to Czar Alexander I of Russia at the end of the Napoleonic wars. From a palace of the House of Savoy came the two tall commodes at the far end of the room; and against the opposite wall two eighteenth-century consoles in gilded wood support a pair of hard-paste porcelain tureens,

Louis XVI drawing room.

Winterhalter's portrait of the Empress Eugénie over the mantel, and cabinets displaying Sèvres china in the drawing room.

The breakfast room.

Opposite, top
The library.

Opposite, bottom
The dining room.

The pavilion.

gilded by the famous Vincent, who could not read or write and signed his name with the number 2,000 (for *vingt-cent,* a play on his French name). The models for these creations are still extant in the factory at Sèvres. Mrs. Post found the finished pieces at different times and in different shops and, in her own words, "had the pleasure of bringing them together again."

A feature of the charming little breakfast room at Hillwood is the bronze chandelier, which was assembled in Saint Petersburg for the Palace of Pavlovsk, and is another significant addition to Mrs. Post's museum collection of Russian and French treasures.

Charles William Post once said of his only daughter, "If Marjorie were cast adrift on a desert isle, she would organize the grains of sand." Her flair for superb organization is exemplified in every area of Hillwood. Each display is cataloged in detail with its history summarized and its time of acquisition carefully noted. Every item at Hillwood, in fact, has a place of its own, carefully charted and recorded. Platters, trays, bowls, and silver service pieces by the dozens, each separately wrapped in plastic, are filed behind a huge

metal door (opened with a combination) in the pantry. Next door is the linen room, where sets of table linens are individually wrapped, tied with satin ribbons, and numbered. The number is duplicated in a book that carries a photograph and description of each set on the shelves. (Upstairs, there is a similar register of all bedroom linens.)

Mrs. Post generously shares the beauties of her estate with her friends when she is in Washington, and also gives innumerable strangers a chance to visit her house and enjoy its collections. Apparently, from the time she bought Hillwood, she envisioned it as something of a museum with treasures that could be enjoyed by many. The general public one day will have that opportunity, for she has willed her palatial estate to the Smithsonian Institution, along with an endowment to maintain it in perpetuity.

Meanwhile, Hillwood, steeped in the elegance that invites not only cultivated appreciation but also relaxed enjoyment, is, indeed, a great house of Washington, as well as the Capital home of one of America's leading hostesses and collectors.

III

PROSPECT HOUSE

Beautifully restored and preserved in the finest Federal or late Georgian tradition, Prospect House at 3508 Prospect Street, Georgetown, is owned by Mrs. Patricia Firestone Chatham.

A twenty-two-room house, dominating 33,000 square feet of land with a view of the Potomac River, the three-story and basement structure has masonry of Flemish bond laid up in bricks that were sand-molded by hand and are now between cherry and chocolate brown in color. The front, with five sizable windows, is neat and artless in effect. The gable roof, flanked by corbeled chimneys, has three dormers with pediments similar to that over the entrance. A sunray fanlight above the front door has small panes which, with lintels of gauged and rubbed brick matching sills and sashes, give the house a light, almost delicate appearance.

Henry Lionel Williams and Ottalie K. Williams, authors of *Great Houses in America,* point out that "Federal houses have the reputation of being both the most sophisticated and the most nearly perfect architectural style developed in the United States." Essentially Federal, the architecture of Prospect House is, indeed, sophisticated in its refinement of tasteful lines and harmonious proportions, and its use of Louis XVI embellishments restrained by elegant American Georgian detail. For example, the general aspect of the façade achieves relaxed dignity by means of such subtle adornments as the decorative cornice, the striking chimneys, and the wrought-iron railings of the front steps.

Later additions to the house, which in no way detract from the validity of its basic style, are the bay windows on the east and, overlooking the terrace, the galleries with their interesting grillwork in grape and leaf designs. Below the rear balcony and on a level with the upper terrace is the patio, another comparatively recent addition. Floored in rough brick, it is big enough to accommodate fifty guests. Hundreds more can be entertained in the gardens, which descend in a series of terraces, patterned with brick walks and English box. The designer was Mina Bruce Haldeman of Glenview, Kentucky, but Mrs. Chatham is responsible for the espaliered peach, apple, and pear trees (she learned the art in Norway) , and the profusion of camellias, azaleas, and

View of Prospect House from the ha-ha wall supporting the upper terrace on the east side.

jonquils that brighten the garden in season. A ha-ha wall supports the upper terraces. The lowest terrace is an unbroken turf sweeping toward the Potomac.

The most unusual feature of the property is the octagonal watchtower or gazebo, from which eighteenth-century owners watched their ships sail into what was once a sea-level port. Built of red brick, the structure is two stories high, fifteen by fifteen feet, with windows on all sides and a pyramidal roof.

In the past, Prospect House has been known by at least three other names. The earliest was Templeman House, which gives the impression that an early owner, John Templeman, built the house. Some authorities have credited William Thornton with designing the dwelling, as he probably would have if his good friend Templeman had indeed been the builder, as the landmark plaque states. But fairly recent authenticated research indicates that the first recorded purchaser was General James McCubbin Lingan, a Revolutionary war hero, who bought the property in 1788 from William Deakins, Jr., one of the commissioners who laid out Georgetown (spelled as two words originally). Lingan now is credited with having had the house built sometime between 1788 and 1793, when he sold it to Templeman.

Templeman hailed from Boston, but he had been in and around Maryland for some time. William Wirt, an author who served as attorney general under Madison and Monroe, mentioned in his *Memoirs* that he saw John Templeman perform on a tight rope with a traveling show in Bladensburg, Maryland, in 1782. One might wonder how he managed to amass enough money to purchase Lingan's house, which must have been the finest dwelling in the "Pretty Prospect" section of what was Montgomery County, Maryland, before 1791. Certain sources hint that there may have been a sinister reason behind Templeman's quick rise to affluence. Almost a century and a half after the house was built, an owner discovered in the course of extensive remodeling an underground tunnel leading to the Potomac. A contemporary account mentioned that the passageway "had huge iron rings on the wall indicating that some ancient owner might have engaged in slave running."

There is no evidence, however, that either Lingan or Templeman was a slave trader. Lingan was a collector for the port of Georgetown in 1790, and later held other important offices. Templeman had many business interests. For several years he ran a store that regularly advertised, "Whiskey, Firkin Butter, Linseed Oil, and Flour" (a firkin of butter was a fifty-six-pound cask). He owned merchant ships, was active in transporting tobacco abroad, and probably spent much of his time in his watchtower, with a spyglass trained on his approaching or departing vessels.

He was also president of the Bank of Columbia, and at one time was a real estate associate of Benjamin Stoddert, builder and resident of Halcyon House, which was near the Templeman residence. With Stoddert and Thomas Law, the husband of Martha Washington's granddaughter, Templeman obtained a charter for the Anacostia Bridge Company from the Maryland Legislature in January, 1797, and he alone spearheaded the completion of the Georgetown Bridge over the Potomac, a project that had been stymied

View from the street showing modern wing.

East façade, overlooking the upper terrace. The octagonal watchtower is off to the left.

for four years. His success in that venture won him a tribute from the *Sentinel of Liberty* in July, 1797: "To the enterprise and perseverance of that most useful and public citizen, John Templeman, who gratuitously engaged in the superintendence of the work at its commencement."

That Templeman was a distinguished civic leader was shown when he figured prominently in President Adams' first visit to the new city of Washington and Georgetown in 1800. Anticipating that visit, the newly appointed Secretary of the Navy Benjamin Stoddert wrote to his friend Templeman from Philadelphia on May 29, 1800:

DEAR SIR:

The Pres. will be in Washington by the time you receive this or a day or two after. He proposes to stay but a little while. I wish he could remain longer. This and other good things will depend on the manner of employing his time. I request therefore that setting Bashfulness at defiance you will urge the Pres. to go to the balls, to ride with you in your coach, and to get Mr. Scott at least to go with you. Let the Pres. be pleased with your attention and with the country.

I am resp. yrs.

BEN STODDERT

Barring an accident I expect to be in George-Town the 14th of June.

Templeman complied. "Setting Bashfulness at defiance," he received President Adams in his home, escorted him by coach all over Washington and Georgetown, and accompanied him to the big dinner honoring the distinguished visitor at the Union Tavern. It was this affair that Mrs. William Thornton referred to in her diary of June 3, 1800: "Dr. Thornton went to George Town at two o'clock to dine with the President and inhabitants at the Tavern. The President went away from the dinner before sunset."

He was lucky to escape that early, in view of a report the following week in the *Sentinel of Liberty* that "there were seventeen regular and two volunteer toasts drunk and the utmost harmony and conviviality prevailed." The President's toast, according to the account, was: "To George Town, may its prosperity equal the ardent enterprise of its inhabitants and the felicity of their situation."

From 1800 to 1830, Templeman House attracted many notable visitors, including Lafayette in 1824.

Authorities differ as to when the property passed from the Templeman family. According to some sources, Templeman's widow and then their descendants kept the estate until 1858, when they sold it to Dr. Thomas T. Mann; but it is known that W. H. Whitton bought it in 1861, and that Franklin Steele was a subsequent owner.

Mrs. Steele, a granddaughter of Commodore Joshua Barney and Samuel Chase, was a fabulous hostess, and under her aegis parties at what was called the Templeman-Steele House made social history.

The Steeles had three daughters—Mrs. Arthur Addison, Mrs. Edward McCauley, and Mrs. George Upham Morris. Mrs. Morris inherited the house and lived there many years.

Her husband, Commander Morris, was a Civil War hero. He was the captain of the *Cumberland,* the thirty-gun sailing sloop, when she was rammed by the Confederate ironclad *Merrimac* in Hampton Roads in 1862. Although the *Cumberland* was sunk, Morris was acclaimed for saving most of his men and himself.

He was the son of Commodore Charles Morris, a prominent Georgetown resident, who served courageously in the War with Tripoli and the War of 1812, and was a close friend of Lafayette. George Morris' sister, Louise, disappointed her family very much when she eloped with an obscure bank clerk, W. W. Corcoran, but in time they were delighted to have him in the family, for he became Washington's most distinguished citizen and most generous philanthropist.

Commander and Mrs. Morris made a number of alterations in the Templeman-Steele House, which gradually came to be known as the Morris House. A flat Victorian roof was added onto the structure to support another story, the dormers were put on and the chimneys extended, and a number of Victorian touches were incorporated into the interior.

After Commander Morris died in 1874, his widow continued to live in the house until 1917, often complaining toward the end that the construction of the Capital Transit Company on M Street shook the foundation of her abode and endangered her life.

Under the terms of her will, the property after her death went to the First Spiritualist Church, which had difficulty in maintaining both the house and grounds. The estate was sadly in need of repair when the late Mrs. Morris' nephew, Captain Edward McCauley, a member of the Maritime Commission, took it over in 1934. He and his wife immediately started restoring it, with John W. Adams as the architect. Under a past owner— probably Mrs. Morris—the brick had been stuccoed and painted. The covering was removed to expose the beautiful brick once more. A two-story gallery with lacy grillwork was added to the rear; the twin sitting rooms on the east were combined into a large double drawing room; and Georgian mantels corresponding to the period of the house replaced the arched Italian mantels that the Morrises had installed. Captain McCauley also had the old coach house on the west transformed into a three-car garage with a service wing above. He discovered the underground passageway with the slave rings on the walls, and closed it off.

Commander and Mrs. W. D. Thomas occupied the house in 1938–1939. Patrick J. Hurley, at one time President Hoover's Secretary of War and later United States Ambassador to China, leased it in 1940. Two years later, Sydney A. Mitchell of New York bought the property, and in 1945 he sold it to Josephine Ogden Forrestal, wife of James E. Forrestal, Secretary of the Navy and later the first Secretary of Defense.

Mrs. Forrestal furnished the house with Aubusson rugs, Sheraton, Chippendale, and Duncan Phyfe pieces, and art objects from France. In the dining room, she hung eighteenth-century handpainted Zuber wallpaper, which she also used to cover a ten-foot screen. She added Hepplewhite and Sheraton chairs, antique mahogany sideboards (circa 1780), and a sturdy Duncan Phyfe center table that seats eighteen.

In the drawing room, she placed two Récamier chaise longues, a large Aubusson rug, a satinwood sofa upholstered in gold, a tripod Regency table cut down to coffee-table height, and a magnificent Irish crystal chandelier.

The bedrooms on the second floor were decorated to carry out the architectural theme of the exterior, with a four-poster canopied bed, cushioned chairs, and antiques giving an Early American atmosphere to the master bedroom. The guest bedrooms and suites are similarly furnished.

During the early days of Armed Forces unification, the house was a popular gathering place for high officials, and the target of some gossip. Secretary Forrestal declined to publicize his guest lists, and speculations were rife as to exactly who attended his off-the-record dinners—and why. Among those frequently present, however, was Representative Thurmond Chatham, of North Carolina, a captain in the Naval Reserve, a member of the Foreign Affairs Committee, and a longtime friend of the Defense Secretary.

The dining room, with Zuber wallpaper.

After Forrestal's death in 1949, his widow leased the house to the government. Extensive renovation had begun at the White House, and President and Mrs. Truman had moved into Blair House with the expectation of staying at least two years. The State Department took over Mrs. Forrestal's house, officially named it Prospect House, and ran it until 1951. Visiting notables who stayed there during that period included the Shah of Iran, President M. Vincent Auriol of France, Field Marshal Montgomery, and several Latin American presidents.

After President and Mrs. Truman moved back into the refurbished Executive Mansion, Mrs. Forrestal sold Prospect House and most of the furnishings to Representative and Mrs. Chatham.

In 1951, the new owners at once began extensive work on the house and grounds. They brought box and azalea plants from North Carolina; had formal gardens laid out, terraced, planted, and manicured; modernized the kitchen; remodeled the west wing; added their own collections of furniture, prints, and paintings to those purchased from the Forrestals; and made the estate in general what it is today.

Intent on having a comfortable, homelike atmosphere in a house grand enough to be a museum, Mrs. Chatham turned the largest room on the ground floor into a cozy sitting room that could also serve as the repository for Representative Chatham's collection of books and hunting prints. This spacious, green-walled library now has inviting contemporary sofas and chairs, and a circular, carved coffee table in front of the Adam fireplace. Hunting and sailing prints intersperse the bookshelves that line the walls from floor to ceiling. The one antique in the room is Mrs. Chatham's prize possession—a stalwart mahogany desk that once belonged to General Thomas

Mahogany sideboard in the dining room.

Jonathan (Stonewall) Jackson. (She has willed it to the old Salem restoration project in Winston-Salem, North Carolina.) On the lower floor, also, is the television room, which once served as Secretary Forrestal's office, with cables to the White House and the Pentagon.

Today the double drawing room with its two large bay windows, its twin Adam mantels, and its Irish glass chandelier (the candles are lighted for special occasions) is further enhanced by Sir Joshua Reynolds' painting "Master William Trenchard," which hangs over the satinwood sofa. Sheer glass curtains and raspberry silk taffeta draperies are at the windows. The wide pine floorboards are waxed to a dark mellow glow.

An antique gold Persian rug is in the front hallway, where, on the right of the entrance, stands a tall English chest-on-chest. A gas chandelier hangs from the ceiling, and a lamp with an alabaster globe graces a rosewood table near the understated staircase.

Mrs. Chatham owns all the land to the rear of the house. With four landscaped terraces and a rolling greensward, the property extends to M Street and includes a three-bedroom guest house and all the property that John Templeman bought from General Lingan—120 feet on M (then Fall) Street, 240 feet on Thirty-fifth (then Fayette) Street, and the original frontage on Prospect Street.

The watchtower is still there, a picturesque landmark of Georgetown. A catwalk leads from the dining room to the tower, and the latter also opens onto the lower terrace of the garden.

Ground-floor sitting room.

Now a widow, with grown sons, Mrs. Chatham would like to sell Prospect House with most of its furnishings, and she is hopeful of finding a buyer who will appreciate its treasured beauty and will preserve it accordingly. For Prospect House, a Federal gem of Georgetown, is one of America's few historic dwellings in which a period in complete conformity with the exterior has been successfully re-created and gracefully adapted to modern living.

The double drawing room.

IV

EVERMAY

On a commanding level, yet almost hidden from the street by a mellow brick wall, Evermay in Georgetown is a restored beauty that fulfills the promise of its name and gracefully coordinates the treasured past with the present.

The magnificent manor house, the home of Captain Peter Belin, USN (Ret.), and Mrs. Belin at 1623 Twenty-eighth Street, is in the late Georgian tradition, conforming nicely to modern living in a setting of graduated terraces and lush gardens, burgeoning with restoration planting at its finest. Like most houses built in the eighteenth century, the dwelling itself has undergone a number of architectural changes in the past century and a half, but it stands today as an elegant tribute to the vision and taste of an American diplomat with a rare appreciation of history and the means to restore and preserve a beautiful symbol of it.

He was F. Lammot Belin, the fifth owner of the estate, according to a bronze plaque put up on the walls of the grounds in 1950 by the Colonial Dames of America. A native of Scranton, Pennsylvania, he studied architecture and engineering at Yale, from which he was graduated in 1901. Landscaping was one of his hobbies; collecting was another. One of his intimates once said of him: "He collects continually—oriental effects, watches, bibelots . . . and friends." He had many opportunities to indulge his acquisitive inclinations, as he served in the diplomatic corps from 1917 to 1933. He had been *en poste* in Peking, Constantinople, London, Paris, and at the Lausanne Conference before he bought Evermay in 1923, and later he was Ambassador to Poland.

Many effects in the house today, as well as the imposing forecourt, the sunken garden, and the statuary on the grounds, attest to his flair for acquiring splendid furnishings and ideas from many sources in America and abroad, and also to his ability to bring them together in an elegant edifice, restored and surrounded by grounds far more beautiful than the original owner could ever have envisioned.

Most authorities agree that Evermay was built in 1798. But a diary written by an early resident of Georgetown and recently published by *The Georgetowner* has as a November 14, 1792, entry: "Samuel Davidson is

The south façade of Evermay, originally the front of the house.

building a rather large house with the money he received from the sale of his lots in the Federal City. He calls it 'Evermay'—a very quaint and pretty name."

Samuel Davidson, an irascible, red-haired Scotsman, was one of the commissioners appointed to lay out Georgetown. Like several of his contemporaries, he purchased from Thomas Beall a part of his inherited 408-acre Rock of Dumbarton tract, which became the site of the fledgling city.

A prominent realtor by 1790, Davidson had dabbled in several businesses in previous years. Arriving from Scotland in 1766, he first made his home in Annapolis, where his brother John ran a store and was also deputy collector of the port. Judging from contemporary references, John was a dour, tightfisted but solid citizen, while one account describes Samuel as "light-hearted, free, generous, and impulsive." The first three characteristics were hardly in keeping with those he showed in later life, but "impulsive" he obviously was, for he suddenly gave up working in his brother's store and took to the road as a traveling salesman. Shortly afterward, he was off to Madeira to buy wine, but this venture was unsuccessful. Having lost his cargo in a shipwreck on the way back, he returned to Georgetown determined to go into some other business.

He tried real estate. He knew Thomas Jefferson slightly, and Pierre Charles L'Enfant rather well, and it is quite possible that at some casual meeting with one or both of them at Suter's Tavern, he learned of plans for a President's Square in the Federal city.

At any rate, Davidson teamed up with David Burns, an active speculator, and together they acquired from the Pierce family several hundred acres in the area being considered for the President's Square, and sold it to the government at a nice profit. The land was to become the locale of both Lafayette Square and the White House; and it was with his part of proceeds from the sale that Samuel Davidson purchased the site for Evermay.

The original tract was extensive, reaching from what is now the south side of the United States Treasury building to the present west boundary of Evermay and south to Stoddert (now Q) Street. John Davidson was also in the real estate business by this time. He owned extensive acreage east of his brother's, but apparently both men had some difficulty with persons responsible for planning the Federal city. In a May, 1792, letter to John, who was still living in Annapolis, Samuel told of the deposing of L'Enfant as the principal planner of Washington, and complained about one of his successors as follows: "The darned fool is going to lay out a street from E Street on the north, through my swamp and your woods to the site of your back door. Come here at once and stop him."

Before Evermay was finished, Davidson must have run short of funds. Significantly, the bricks on the south facade, then the front of the house, are much more smoothly laid than the ones on the north entrance.

Davidson was a plagued man on many accounts. Uninvited sportsmen shot game on his premises. Stray dogs bayed at his windows. Undisciplined youths climbed his fence and plundered his fruit trees. Young men and women of questionable character consorted under his groves, and utter

The belvedere, overlooking the lower garden.

strangers knocked at his door and begged permission to see the inside of his mansion. When even his neighbors began to intrude on his privacy, he took an unprecedented step and placed a paid advertisement in a local publication of June 2, 1810, with this headline:

Evermay proclaims,
Take care, enter not here,
For punishment is near.

Continuing, the notice warned:

At their peril, all persons, of whatever age, color, or standing in society, from trespassing on the premises in any manner, by day or by night; particularly all thieving knaves and idle vagabonds; all rambling parties; all assignation parties; all amorous bucks with their doxies, and all sporting bucks with their dogs and guns.

Not one to discourage contacts that might be profitable, however, Davidson concluded his advertisement as follows:

For the information of those persons who have real business on the premises, there is a good and convenient gate. But Mark! I do not admit mere curiosity as an errand of business. Therefore, I beg and pray of all neighbors to avoid Evermay as they would a den of devils, or rattle snakes, and thereby save themselves and me much vexation and trouble.

Whether that stern warning had its desired effect is not now known; but no other similar notice appeared. Presumably, the eccentric bachelor spent the rest of his life in the solitude he sought, or in the company of his nephew Lewis Grant.

Grant came over from Scotland and settled in Georgetown in 1798, but he was looking after a store in Prince George's County, Maryland, when Davidson's will was executed in December, 1805. It bequeathed Evermay to Grant, on condition that he take the name of Davidson. Six other relatives were named alternates to Lewis Grant. In case all refused, the will expressed the hope that "They may all go to heaven in their own way," and stipulated that the estate was to be sold, with the proceeds going "to found a college for poor white boys on the frontier"—the frontier then being Ohio.

Grant, however, promptly added Davidson to his name. His only daughter became Eliza Grant Davidson, and both of them moved to Evermay. Samuel Davidson's last will and testament also requested that the portion of the property containing his grave "be the last part of my estate . . . that should be sold."

It was Eliza who, after her marriage, presided over the liquidation of two thirds of the original Evermay estate and saw that Davidson's injunction was carried out. In conveying twelve and a half acres to the adjoining Oak Hill Cemetery some time between 1851 and 1878, she retained the title to the "square of 24 feet of ground" designated as Davidson Circle in the official records of the cemetery. The cemetery had been chartered by Congress in 1949, with William W. Corcoran donating most of the land. To this day, Davidson's descendants have keys to the cemetery's private gate, which is near the present north wall bordering Evermay.

Reverting to Eliza Grant Davidson, Evermay was brought into the expansive Dodge fold through her marriage to Charles Dodge. The marriage created a sensation in Georgetown.

Charles was the son of Francis Charles Dodge, who had considerable shipping and realty interests, and lived with his wife and eleven offspring at Dodge Farm, a spacious house on the southeast corner of Q and Thirty-first streets. Francis Dodge was a patriarch accustomed to having his own way, even when it went against convention. For example, convention then, as now, decreed that a wedding should take place either in a church or at the home of the bride's parents or another of her relatives. But with two sons and two daughters on the verge of marriage, it seemed eminently fitting to Francis Dodge that they should all be married at the same time, in his house and at an hour most convenient for their prompt departure afterward.

Accordingly, the four young couples exchanged vows in a multiple ceremony in the living room of Dodge Farm on June 12, 1847, at 4 A.M. so all the newlyweds could board the once-a-day stage to Baltimore. In addition to Charles Dodge and Eliza Davidson, the couples thus united and dispatched were Allen Dodge and Mary Ellen Barry, Adeline Dodge and Charles Lanham, and Virginia Dodge and Benjamin Perley Poore.

Five of Charles Dodge's progeny built homes near Dodge Farm, so that several blocks in Georgetown had a Dodge house. Even the name of Evermay was eclipsed for a time and became known as just "another Dodge house," which must have delighted Francis Dodge.

In time, Charles and Eliza had reason to be glad that his father was pleased with them. He left them a substantial inheritance. He also left a strange document addressed to Charles and beginning as follows:

If you wish to appear decent, shave every morning below the ears and nose, cut your hair short all over your head, wear white cravats, no bootstraps or pantaloon straps.

Echoing the advice of Shakespeare's Polonius to his son, the annotation also stressed the dangers of borrowing and lending, the value of safeguarding worthy friendships, and the importance of courageously bearing any unavoidable quarrel.

The Dodges made few changes in the appearance of Evermay. During the Civil War, however, the Dodge fortune dwindled, and the house was very much in need of repair when Charles and Eliza sold it to John D. McPherson in 1877, and went to live in a frame house opposite the Thirty-first Street gate of Tudor Place.

A member of the prosperous firm of McPherson & Carlisle, the new owner was prepared to spend money on the property—and did. The house soon bore little resemblance to what it had originally been; Victorian additions and refurbishing gave it a different character. Gingerbread adorned what had been a simple cupola. There were haphazard balconies and a small pillared porch on the south façade, then the entrance, all in keeping with an era that spawned architectural frills. A sleeping porch was built over the west wing, and yellow paint covered the rose brick exterior.

In 1897, the name of John D. McPherson disappeared from the City Directory, and the listing for Evermay showed "Frances W. McPherson, widow of John D." as the owner. But within a year, she moved to Chevy Chase and leased Evermay to William Baxley Orme, prominent in civic and social circles and an official of the Washington Gas Light Company.

The move to Evermay was something of a homecoming for Mrs. Orme. The former Julia Lockwood, she was a daughter of Colonel and Mrs. Henry Hayes Lockwood. The Lockwoods had lived at Evermay from 1876 to 1877, and Julia had many happy memories of it. In 1879, she became the bride of William Orme; they had a thriving family by the time they moved to Evermay in 1898. They were to continue leasing the estate from McPherson landlords until 1919, and during their tenancy it figured more prominently than ever before in the social and literary life of Georgetown. Gregarious and popular, Mr. and Mrs. Orme entertained often, and invitations to their soirees for celebrated authors were prized.

On March 28, 1905, Mrs. Orme invited thirty-five prominent women to tea for the specific purpose of organizing a group to promote appreciation of the arts and sciences. The result was The Evermay Club. Its constitution stated that the objects of the club "Shall be the study of the civilized nations more especially as regards their literature, arts, architecture, and handicrafts: second, the consideration of current events in politics, history, arts, science and religion."

The oldest literary group in Washington, The Evermay Club is still going strong. Its active membership remains limited to thirty-five; regular meetings are held on every third Thursday of the month from October through May, exclusive of December, at 11 A.M.; the annual fee is traditionally two dollars; each meeting features "a paper," by a member; and the original motto has been retained: "Unity in work creates power."

An active member is Mrs. J. Carter Fort, the former Eloise Orme, who moved with her parents to Evermay when she was four years old, and was reared and married there.

Today, Mrs. Fort recalls the constant social activity at Evermay, and particularly that in connection with her own wedding, a garden event in June, 1917. She took her vows kneeling on the trysting stone on the southeast side of the house.

Mrs. Fort also vividly remembers that the estate was quite different in appearance from what it is today. There was a turn-around driveway at the south entrance. What is now a large drawing room was divided by Grecian pillars into a music room on the north and a parlor on the south. Across the center hall were a dining room on the south and a library on the north. A door to the pantry led inconveniently from the library, instead of from the

Rare Chinese effects in the stately dining room.

dining room. On the second floor were five bedrooms and a bath with a tin-lined wooden tub. There were two additional rooms in the wing, and two large chambers on the third floor.

Mrs. Fort also recalls that the family spent one summer away from Washington and sublet Evermay for three months to Prince David, brother of Hawaiian Queen Liliuokalani, and his family.

While the Ormes lived at Evermay, the small structure on the northwest side, originally a smokehouse, was enlarged for use as a stable. An inveterate gardener, Mrs. Orme planted the white wisteria that still climbs over the south façade. Also, she planted four copper beech trees on the east before she could get one to grow. It is still there.

Not long after World War I, the splendid site of Evermay and its commercial possibilities attracted the attention of Francis E. Duehay, a onetime superintendent of United States prisons and former hotel owner and operator. In 1919, he purchased Evermay from the McPherson estate with the expectation of razing the house and building a residential hotel on the property.

The contemplated project followed a trend toward the indiscriminate construction of hotels and small apartment buildings all over the District of Columbia. There were no zoning laws to regulate height or style, and some sixty thousand persons, during World War I, had stayed on to settle permanently in the Federal city, which was unprepared to house them.

Duehay's plan to replace Evermay with a luxurious hotel, however, met with strong opposition from the Georgetown Citizens Association, which saw the proposed commercial structure as a threat to the residential character of the area. The group moved quickly and in October, 1923, succeeded in persuading the newly established Zoning Commission to bar, temporarily, the building of multiple dwelling units in Georgetown.

Duehay did not care to gamble on whether the commission might one day lift the ban. He put Evermay on the market. Meanwhile, members of the Citizens Association had been looking for someone who might buy the property for continued use as a home. They found their answer in F. Lammot Belin, and persuaded him to look at the estate. He visited it for the first time on November 28, the day before Thanksgiving in 1923, and promptly purchased it.

In May of the following year, the construction code recommended by the Citizens Association was officially incorporated into the District of Columbia's zoning regulations. Several distinguished residences were saved by the ruling: "No building shall be erected for an apartment, or a hotel, nor shall any existing buildings be enlarged for these purposes in Georgetown."

Meanwhile, Belin had begun an extensive renovation program, designed to restore the late Georgian style of the house and to create an appropriate setting. Nine coats of yellow paint were removed from the exterior, uncovering the original old-rose brick. The ornate front porch on the south was ripped off, and the south driveway was removed to make way for terraces with hazel hedges, statuary fountains, and picturesque walks, bordered with Virginia box and azalea beds. The elaborate garden plan also took into careful account the deciduous magnolias already on the grounds, as well as the white dogwood trees and the enormous cedars and elms, and the oldest plant on the premises, a holly tree that dates back at least two centuries. A brick wall went up on the Twenty-eighth Street side of the estate, and the stable was replaced with a gatehouse and garage.

Many features of the house show the influence of Ambassador Belin's sojourns abroad. The sunken reflecting pool with a fountain and the rows of columns surrounding the lower garden in peristyle effect are reminiscent of one he had seen in Rabat, Morocco. The belvedere with its white Doric pillars supporting a soft green dome could adorn any Old World garden. At the foot of the lower terrace is a moon gate, a lacy reminder of Mr. Belin's tour of duty in Peking.

A grove of trees today softens the approach to the north entrance, which faces a magnificent octagonal forecourt, paved with rose-colored Belgian blocks in a swirl pattern. The center fountain in a lotus design was executed by Milles, the famous Swedish sculptor. The wall of the forecourt describes a graceful curve from five feet six at the highest to three feet six at the lowest. The north entrance to the house is a model of Georgian splendor, with a paneled doorway framed by a semicircular hood, sidelights, a low stoop, newel lamps, and an iron handrail.

Ivy climbs the walls of the house and terraces. A tennis court and a vegetable garden are on the east. Over the box hedge on the east and toward the south one can see the city of Washington in panorama, including the Capitol dome.

Ambassador Belin installed new plumbing at Evermay and completely redecorated the interior, making it one of the loveliest homes in Washington today. Old English paneling, with a carved cornice in the spacious drawing room, provides a rich background for Hoppner portraits, cabinets displaying a jade collection, and taffeta curtains repeating the blue of the Chippendale sofa.

The dining room, with its twin mantels as reminders that it originally was two rooms, now extends the entire width of the house. Richly paneled in teakwood, it has an enormous Gobelin tapestry—unusual because of its Chinese motif—a lacquer cabinet from Peking, and a Coromandel screen which once might have adorned the palace of an oriental potentate.

An exquisite silver epergne, similar to the famous one in the Governor's Palace at Colonial Williamsburg, graces a sideboard. The exceptional plaques on the east wall, of inlaid pearl on dark metal and Chinese characters in red, are ancient Chinese calling cards, which notables sent ahead of their visits to distinguished residents of ancient Peking.

While Evermay was being restored in the 1920's, an enormous old walnut tree was removed to make way for the terraces on the south grounds. Twenty-five years later, a workman informed Ambassador Belin that he still had the wood. It now floors the dining room in wide, waxed boards.

From the moment Ambassador Belin bought Evermay, he planned to add a wing on the east to balance the one near Twenty-eighth Street. First,

he built a sunroom with two windows on the south and three on the east. Later, he enlarged the area with another window on the south. Then, while visiting England, he admired an orangery in a country house and decided to transform the sunroom at Evermay.

Patterned after the conservatory at Wye House in Maryland, the orangery was completed in 1960, about a year before his death. Today, it is a lovely, living monument to him. Two stories high, the twenty-six by forty-one-foot room has rose brick walls enclosing orange trees, evergreens, and climbing fig vines. The inspiration for the enormous fireplace with the curved top came from one at Dower House, the Maryland estate of the late Mrs. Eleanor (Cissy) Patterson. A Japanese screen over the fireplace, two handsome Korean cabinets, and Chinese Chippendale furniture from the early Manchu dynasty decorate this room, the bay windows of which overlook the patio.

There are five bedchambers on the second and third floors. Particularly inviting is the upstairs sitting room, paneled with walnut brought from Avignon, and containing a seventeenth-century gold and blue Chinese rug.

After the death of Ambassador Belin on July 6, 1961, Evermay went to his son, Captain Peter Belin, USN (Ret.), who with his wife lives there today, maintaining this great house in a manner befitting its exceptional history and its unimpeachable elegance.

The sunroom, patterned
after the conservatory
at Wye House in
Maryland.

V

WORTHINGTON HOUSE

Named after a distinguished nineteenth-century owner, who called it Quality Hill, Worthington House at 3425 Prospect Street is the Georgetown home of Senator and Mrs. Claiborne Pell. As a tribute to both the distinguished area in which it was located and the elegance of the house itself, Dr. Charles Worthington chose its first name shortly after he purchased it in 1810. The property continued to be known as Quality Hill for almost half a century—for as long as he and his family lived there, in fact. Then, oddly enough, Worthington's name became attached to it and has remained ever since.

There is nothing pretentious about the structure on the corner of Prospect and Thirty-fifth (formerly Fayette) streets. Flush with the sidewalk of the corner site, it is nicely proportioned, with three stories and a high basement, dormers, a colonial doorway, sandstone steps with a wrought-iron rail on either side, and twenty-four-pane windows. The functional interior features a seventy-foot-wide hall, with the library and dining room on the right of the entrance. Notable in these rooms are the original cornice and frieze, selected by the builder. The spacious sitting room, its woodwork beautifully restored, is on the left of the hall. A broad, curved stairway leads to the upper floors. An ell-shaped area accommodating the kitchen, pantry, and servants' quarters adjoins the walled garden to the rear.

The coordinated appearance of the house today gives the impression that it was lifted intact out of the past; but, like most restored dwellings dating to the eighteenth century, it has survived several alterations.

Fortunately, the owner-builder was a man of cultivated tastes, with enough money to plan a house that could withstand the ravages of time. He was John Thomson Mason, of Analostan (now Theodore Roosevelt) Island, a nephew of George Mason of Gunston Hall, an intimate friend of Washington's and author of the Bill of Rights. In 1780, John Mason became the first attorney admitted to the bar in Montgomery County, Maryland. He served for a time as attorney for the District of Columbia, but turned down other government posts later. His absorbing interest centered around his stable of blooded horses, which he inherited along with considerable acreage in both

Stafford and Prince William counties. He was also engaged in shipping tobacco, and his sailing vessels returning from abroad brought much of the building materials and some of the furnishings for the house he built on Prospect Street in 1798. From England came the bricks which were laid in Flemish bond for the exterior. Today they are barely discernible beneath layers of gray paint.

The classic front doorway was styled with slender colonnettes and surmounted by a graceful pediment. The modillions and a fluted frieze were designed to follow the line of the eaves across the gable ends.

An admirable structure outside and in, the dwelling must have pleased Mason, but it could not lure him long from his country estate. In 1807, he sold the house to John Teackle, described in a periodical of the day as "a man of fortune from the Eastern Shore of Virginia."

With daughters of marriageable age, Teackle probably was well aware that their chances of attracting desirable suitors would be much better if the family was ensconced in Georgetown rather than on a secluded Virginia estate, no matter how luxurious; so, early in 1807, he moved to his new home and began an active calendar of party-giving there. That Teackle's program was successful in regard to at least one daughter was indicated in a letter from socially impeccable Mrs. Josiah Quincy to a friend in New York in September, 1810. She referred to the eldest of the Teackle girls as:

> . . . one who would be thought of as a fine woman anywhere, but here she is a treasure—religious, sensible, with a mind highly cultivated and pleasing manners, and though not handsome, her countenance is expressive of uncommon acuteness and observation. All these qualities have not escaped the notice of Mr. Elihu Chauncey, to whom she is engaged, and who will soon take her to Philadelphia, to the regret of her friends here.

The library.

The young couple exchanged wedding vows in the house on October 13, 1810. Twenty select friends witnessed the ceremony in the parlor (today, the sitting room). John Teackle must have felt that his mission in Georgetown was fulfilled, for he sold the property and returned to Virginia before the end of the year.

Dr. Worthington, the next owner, was an unusual man with a notable background. The son of Nicholas Worthington and the grandson of John Worthington—both distinguished men—Charles Worthington won acclaim on his own. He was awarded hundreds of acres in Anne Arundel County, Maryland, for "valor beyond the line of duty," in defending Annapolis against the Indians.

He was graduated with a medical degree from the University of Pennsylvania in 1782, and shortly thereafter moved to a dwelling on the corner of Bridge (now M) and Market (now Thirty-third) streets in Georgetown. Then he bought the house on Prospect Street, took up residence there, and promptly named the place Quality Hill.

Dr. Worthington's medical practice flourished; so did his civic and social

activities—and his wardrobe. Described by a contemporary as "an austere man, full of devoting himself to his profession and to all good works with constancy and patience," he was also a devotee of fashion. He wore his powdered hair in a queue to set off a frilled waistcoat, a fitted coat, knee breeches, and silk stockings above silver buckled shoes; and, when making professional or social calls, he rode in a splendid coach-and-four.

In his day, physicians generally visited the ill in their homes, but Dr. Worthington often administered to patients at Quality Hill, where he had an office and a two-room hospital on the second floor. It was there that he treated some of the British officers who were wounded at the Battle of Bladensburg. According to a contemporary record, he "so won the hearts of the English by his hospitality and skillful care that one of the officers shortly afterward presented him with a gold snuffbox."

His aid to soldiers who had been fighting his own countrymen was not surprising. Like many other prominent Georgetown citizens, Dr. Worthington was an avowed Federalist, and at first openly opposed to "Mr. Madison's War," as the War of 1812 was called by many. But when he received the snuffbox, he probably had to summon all his diplomacy to accept it; for by that time the British, after routing the outnumbered American forces at Bladensburg on the evening of August 24, 1814, had marched on undefended Washington, burned the Capitol and the White House, and destroyed most remaining loyalties to the Crown in the area.

Quality Hill for many years was a popular meeting place for civic leaders and the socially elite, among whom Dr. Worthington was increasingly prominent. He was one of the founders of St. John's Church, Georgetown, and many times chairman of the George Washington Birthnight Ball at Union Tavern. He also helped to organize the Medical and Chirurgical Faculty of Maryland, and was the first president of the District of Columbia Medical Society.

Quality Hill was Dr. Worthington's city home, but he and his family spent much time at their country place, located on what is now Seventh Street, near Brightwood in the District of Columbia. In 1856, he bought a house on Road (now R) Street, Mackall Square, and left Quality Hill unoccupied.

Shortly before the Civil War, Quality Hill was purchased by James Kearney, a wealthy Virginia landowner, who was to live there with his family for many years. He made some alterations on the house. The original tile roof was beginning to disintegrate, so he had it covered with galvanized tin. The room that later was to be a library, opening into the dining room, was a music room for the Kearneys. Dr. Worthington's small office became a closet, where quantities of quinine and other medicines he had left were stored (and where they stayed until 1939, when the closet was made into a powder room), and the doctor's hospital became a master bedroom.

Louise, James Kearney's youngest daughter, was born there in 1872. When Louise Kearney de Yturbide died in an Arlington, Virginia, hospital at the age of ninety-five, her obituary on September 17, 1967, recalled the time and place of her birth and her marriage to Agustín de Yturbide,

Family portraits and antiques in the dining room.

The colonial hallway, as seen from the main entrance.

grandson and namesake of the man who was proclaimed emperor of Mexico in 1822.

The Yturbide story was a sensation in nineteenth-century Georgetown. The Mexican emperor, whose name was originally spelled Iturbide, abdicated in March, 1823, and fled to Europe, while his family sought asylum in the United States and settled in Georgetown. Returning to Mexico on July 15, 1824, he was shot. His wife and his son, called Prince Iturbide, stayed on in Georgetown, and the young man married General Uriah Forrest's granddaughter, Alice Green. Years later, their son, Agustín de Yturbide II, was adopted by Ferdinand Maximilian, when he became emperor of Mexico, and was designated heir to the throne. But when Agustín's widowed mother, then living in Mexico, learned that the arrangement called for her return to the United States, never again to see her son, she spirited him out of Mexico, and they took up residence in Georgetown.

The move probably saved the boy's life. Victorious forces under the insurgent Juárez soon ended the second Mexican empire, and brought about Maximilian's death. Meanwhile, young Agustín entered Georgetown College. Soon after his graduation, he and Miss Kearney were married in a quiet ceremony in Worthington House.

Members of the Kearney family lived there until after World War I. When they moved, Georgetown was no longer the fashionable residential center that it had been for decades—and was destined to be again—and like several other splendid old residences in the area, the place remained vacant for years.

In the late 1920's, it was acquired by Albert Adsit Clemons, who some time before had bought Halcyon House, originally the home of Benjamin Stoddert, at 3400 Prospect Street. It was the eccentric Clemons who was responsible for the grotesque architectural additions to Halcyon House. He perched an outsized Indian figure over the colonial doorway, and placed an Italian gate in front of it. He complicated the façade of the house with illogical balconies and aberrant urns and lamps, and cluttered the interior with a confusing labyrinth of narrow passageways and cut-up rooms.

The sitting room.

Ill health may have been somewhat responsible for Clemons' erraticism. Reputed to have been a hypochondriac even as a young man at Harvard, he moved in a wheelchair during the latter part of his life; and he was obsessed with the fear that he might be buried alive. (His will stipulated that it should be read aloud to relatives any time he became seriously ill; and if he was pronounced dead, his heart should be pierced before the undertaker was summoned.)

Clemons was dabbling in real estate, buying furnishings indiscriminately to add to his nondescript collection, and living at Halcyon House while he owned Worthington House—by then sometimes called the Mason-Worthington House or the Worthington-Kearney House. But each day, he wheeled himself across the street to superintend alterations and additions on his newest property. He put a rail on the garden wall, cleared out the basement, and had the drawing room and main hallway repainted. A theatre buff, he had already built a small auditorium for play productions at

Halcyon House, and he may have considered having another theatre in Worthington House, for he purchased rows upon rows of seats from the old Ford's Theatre and stored them on its third floor.

Serious illness in 1939, however, prompted him to turn the dwelling and its contents over to Harvard; and it remained vacant until Lady Lewis, the wife of Sir Wilmott Lewis, longtime Washington correspondent for the London *Times,* bought it during World War II. Then, despite emergency priorities and vaulting prices, she launched an extensive renovation program to make the old house attractive and livable, while restoring its original character as much as possible.

The place was a virtual wreck when she began. The galvanized tin roof was corrugated and loose, and leakage over the years had ruined most of the walls. She had the roof sheathed with pine and recovered with tile.

Because the third floor had small windows, it was too dark to be used for anything but storage. The resourceful new owner restored the original six dormers to provide light for the three sizable rooms she had built in the attic.

Inside partitions of the house, all of solid brick and originally covered by plaster, were strengthened by hogshair and horsehair. With the exception of those in the drawing room, all the brick walls prior to being replastered had to be furred (leveled and sheathed). The two massive brick arches in the interior presented a problem. In danger of collapsing while the second floor was being renovated, they had to be supported with sturdy beams and smaller arches before they could be permanently reinforced.

All seven fireplaces in the house were relined with fireproof brick. The hallway was paneled and bookcases were added on either side of the mantel-piece in the library. The floors of ponderosa pine had lasted remarkably well, but the wide planks, ranging in length from thirty to forty feet, had to be buttressed at intervals. Oiled and waxed, and covered in part by Lady Lewis' rich Bokhara rugs, the original flooring served nicely.

Central heating, modern plumbing, and seven and a half bathrooms were installed. The basement was raised, and a small apartment was made in it. The two maids' rooms on the second floor of the ell wing were redecorated, as were the bedrooms on the second and third floors. The main kitchen and pantry were modernized.

Lady Lewis haunted auction sales to find the proper appurtenances for her house. She searched assiduously before she finally located, at an estate sale, a chandelier of exactly the right size for the library. Of brass and crystal in a splendid eighteenth-century design, it had originally been made in Scotland; but, styled with arms curving up to form a crown, it looked as if it had been made for the room with its classic cornice and frieze. At the same sale, she obtained sconces for the main hall. At a small antique shop in Virginia she found the brackets for the dining room and used them to flank one of her prized possessions, a handsome mahogany sideboard made for James Monroe when he was Ambassador to France and bearing his profile on the medallion bases of the drawer handles.

Lady Lewis cleared the garden, replanted it, and had magnolia trees espaliered on the west wall. From an antique shop in Georgetown, she purchased two sedate carriage lamps to place at the entrance. She had the house completely repainted and added the white cypress shutters, which are exact copies of the ones chosen by John Mason. The front doorway and the sandstone steps are the originals; and the wide twenty-four-pane windows have most of the glass that was put in when the dwelling was built.

Lady Lewis entertained many celebrated persons during the several years she lived in the house. Then, in 1961, she sold it to Senator and Mrs. Claiborne Pell of Rhode Island. With their two sons, two daughters, and two dogs, the new owners moved in and made the house what it is today, an inviting mélange of family effects, memorabilia, and choice collections.

One of the coziest rooms is the library. Mrs. Pell had the walls painted red, and added red and cream-colored curtains and matching upholstery to provide a cheerful background for portraits, other paintings, and well-worn bric-a-brac. Over the mantelpiece is a portrait by Olive Bigelow Pell, the senator's stepmother. It is of Claiborne Pell as a boy, with his father, Herbert Claiborne Pell, who was a member of Congress from New York and, later, Minister to Portugal and Hungary. Dominating another wall is a study of Alexander James Dallas, the senator's great-great-great-grandfather, who was James Madison's Secretary of the Treasury. (His son, George Mifflin Dallas, was elected Vice President of the United States in 1844, and lived at Decatur House on Lafayette Square during his term of office. As one of the Capital city's most distinguished citizens of his day, he probably was well acquainted with Georgetown's most prominent physician, Dr. Worthington.)

A lovely Madonna and Child, and an assortment of other paintings, sketches, and reproductions are in the library, as are framed decorations which the senator's father received from France, Italy, Portugal, Luxembourg, and Czechoslovakia.

An Olive Bigelow Pell portrait of Herbert Claiborne Pell when he was Minister to Portugal hangs over the mantelpiece in the dining room, where there are also portraits of Senator and Mrs. Pell and each of their children at the age of two, all by Olive Bigelow Pell.

A tureen and tray center the dining-room table, while eight matching pieces—compotes and covered containers—are on the sideboard. The collection once belonged to Mrs. Pell's forebear, General Columbus O'Donnell of Baltimore, who had a flair for acquiring joy-forever things of beauty. Walls of the dining room are cream-colored, and the cotton damask curtains are pale yellow. The crystal chandelier is from Mexico.

Accentuating the historic background of the house is the wide colonial hallway, extending from the entrance to the terrace at the rear. Of special interest in the area opening onto the library on one side and the sitting room on the other is the marble-topped, brass-trimmed Georgian table, surmounted by a Georgian mirror.

The sitting room, like the other rooms in the house, emphasizes comfort and family associations, past and present, rather than impersonal elegance

and rare collections. The cream-colored cotton damask curtains are beautifully draped and fringed. A graceful Chippendale desk in the black and gold Chinese tradition, a grand piano decorated with Chinese motifs, and fine paintings, including George Caleb Bingham's "The Jolly Flatboatmen," attract immediate attention of the connoisseur. But of equal interest to the average visitor are the four extraordinary wax portraits of Senator Pell's ancestors; and, above the mantelpiece, the portrait of Mrs. Pell, the former Nuala O'Donnell, and her brother, Columbus O'Donnell, as children.

In the back hallway, the curved staircase, which has two armored knights on the landing, adjoins a wall covered with an unusual display of etchings. The second floor, where Dr. Worthington once had his office and hospital, now accommodates the master bedroom, adjoined by twin bathrooms, another bedroom, and the senator's book-lined study, in which a vast array of official documents and papers attests that this is the working home office of a dedicated public servant. Also in this room is a display of decorations which Claiborne Pell received from abroad before he was elected to the Senate, and mementos of his extensive travels on official and private fact-finding missions to Cuba, Eastern Europe, Africa, and Asia. (He was a State Department and career American Foreign Service officer for seven years, and has been active in several organizations of global import. For his work as vice president of the International Rescue Committee, he received the Caritas Medal from Franz Cardinal Koenig of Austria and the Order of Merit with Crown from the Knights of Malta, who later awarded him their Grand Cross of Merit. He was made a Knight of the Crown of Italy for his activity in helping to rehabilitate the Sicilian fishing industry. He was also decorated by the government of Portugal, and was awarded the Legion of Honor by France.)

Guarding the door from the main hallway to the terrace are figures of two turbaned blackamoors in yellow attire. The walled garden, beyond, has a picturesque entrance gate, a magnificent magnolia tree and espaliered magnolias on the periphery, a wall fountain, and a statue of Cupid and Psyche.

Leaving the house by the front entrance, one should pause in the small vestibule. The handsome colonial door with its fretted fanlight recalls the era in which the house was built, and there are other noteworthy attractions here. The floor is a giant checkerboard of black and white marble, and the walls on either side feature fascinating pictures, including a colored etching of Iroquois, the first American-born-and-bred horse to win the English Derby. Iroquois captured the cherished trophy, while wearing the cherry and black racing colors of Senator Pell's great-granduncle, Pierre Lorillard, famed founder of Tuxedo Park and a tobacco empire.

Virtually every area in Worthington House has some effect that recalls noted relatives, including a portrait of Sir John Pell, to whom the British Crown granted Pelham Manor in the Hudson Valley in 1687. A distinguished domicile from many standpoints, in fact, this historic Washington house is a serene bulwark against the nervous outside world and a charming memento of the gracious past, quietly blended with the twentieth century.

Senator Pell's study on the second floor.

The terrace to the rear of the house, overlooking the walled garden.

VI

TUDOR PLACE

On the crest of a hill rising from Q Street at Thirty-first sits one of the earliest great houses of Washington, an authentic reminder of Dr. William Thornton's architectural genius, and widely regarded as his masterpiece. It is Tudor Place, the buff stuccoed brick home of Armistead Peter III, great-great-great-great-grandson of Martha Washington.

The estate has belonged to a member of the Peter family since Thomas Peter and his wife, Martha's granddaughter and namesake, acquired it in 1805 and engaged Thornton, the original architect of the Capitol, to design it. Today, the mansion appears very much as it did when it was completed in 1816.

An architectural gem that reflects its colonial antecedents and yet represents a departure from the late Georgian architecture of the preceding century, it presaged the Greek Revival style that was to become the rage around 1820.

Rural rather than urban in type, the eighteen-room dwelling features a unique portico, a large central area set off with wings, fifteen-foot ceilings, and serene, richly mellow rooms with delicate moldings and cornices. In contrast to many other big houses of the era, the general plan illustrates the value of a great hall, minimizes the importance of a staircase, and makes the most of a strikingly beautiful interior as a pleasing backdrop for fine seventeenth- and eighteenth-century furnishings. And its surroundings, studded with box, oak, and maple trees, and including a picturesque garden and indigenous dependencies, are completely in keeping with the manorial tradition.

From its beginning, the estate has been tied in with notable individuals and historic events. Its five and a half acres originally were part of the "Rock of Dumbarton," which belonged to Scottish-born Ninian Beall long before there was a Georgetown.

Beall, shipped to the Colonies as an indentured servant, worked out his sentence on schedule, and in time became chief of the provincial forces of Maryland. In reward for his success in deterring Indian depredations, the Colonial Assembly by order of Queen Anne in 1702 awarded him a grant of

The south facade of Tudor Place, facing Thirty-first Street.

69

759 acres along Rock Creek. It was to be called the "Rock of Dumbarton," after the landmark above the Firth of Clyde in his native Scotland, and a part of it was to become Georgetown, the new community which was incorporated in 1789 and named after George II, the reigning king.

Ninian Beall's son George had inherited the property, and six commissioners appointed by the assembly of the Province of Maryland had completed a survey indicating that the "Rock of Dumbarton," along with "Knaves Disappointment," owned by George Gordon, were the tracts found "most convenient" for the proposed commercial and residential center.

When each owner was offered two town lots plus the price of condemnation, Gordon fell in with the plan at once and joined the group dedicated to persuading the reluctant Beall to agree. He finally acquiesced, but with reluctance. "I do hereby protest and declare," he said, "that my acceptance of the said lots which is by force, shall not debar me from future redress from the Commissioners or others, if I can have the rights of a British subject. God save the King."

On his death in 1780, the property passed to his son Thomas, who four years later sold eight acres of it to Francis Lowndes, a prosperous shipping merchant.

In time, Lowndes built on the property twin, two-story structures, locating them far enough apart so that a large dwelling could be constructed between them. But his dreams of a mansion there were not to be realized. His shipping profits declined. Finally, he gave up the idea of building a bigger house, and in 1805 he sold the estate to Thomas Peter and his wife, the former Martha ("Patty") Parke Custis.

Thomas Peter was a well-to-do young man, the son of Robert Peter from Garn Kirke, Scotland, who served as the first mayor of Georgetown, and was a close friend of George Washington.

Thomas and Patty Peter had been married ten years when they bought the property. Following their wedding in January, 1795, at Abingdon-on-the-Potomac, they had lived in a house built for them at 2618 K Street, just east of Rock Creek. George Washington, on his many trips north from Mount Vernon, often stayed there, and a bronze plaque on the house before it was demolished in 1961 read: "George Washington was a guest in this house on his last night in the city, August 5, 1799." He died the following December.

Patty Peter naturally wanted a home that could compare favorably with Mount Vernon, where she had spent much time before her marriage; Arlington Mansion, which was built by her brother, George Washington Parke Curtis; and Woodlawn Plantation, the rosy brick mansion that George and Martha Washington gave to Patty's sister Eleanor ("Nelly") Parke Curtis, when she married Major Fielding Lewis, George Washington's nephew.

Shortly after Thomas and Martha Peter acquired the Lowndes estate, they moved into the house on the east, used the one on the west as a stable and coach house, and engaged Dr. William Thornton to design the central portion of a mansion, for which the two original structures could serve as wings.

The starkly simple doorway of the north entrance.

Versatile Dr. Thornton, already famous, was the logical choice as architect. His design for the national Capitol not only had won the 1793 competition, but also impressed both President Washington and Secretary of State Jefferson to the extent that they insisted, despite strenuous objections, that it be followed to the final detail. At Jefferson's invitation, Thornton had also made preliminary sketches for the University of Virginia, which were used in part. He had been the architect for the main portion of Madison's Virginia mansion, Montpelier, and of Woodlawn Plantation, south of Alexandria. In the Federal city, Thornton had drawn plans for the residence of Thomas Law, the sometimes wealthy but generally profligate Englishman who married Martha Peter's elder sister, Eliza. Probably more to the point, Thornton had planned The Octagon, the finest residence in the city of Washington, for Colonel John Tayloe, owner of the vast Mount Airy estate in Virginia.

Thornton made innumerable preliminary plans for Tudor Place. The present owner has a fascinating series of the architect's drawings, which originally indicated four large, oval rooms on the first floor. Later designs show a large oval area as the axis of the house, along with a main entrance from the south portico, a handsome stairway on the west side entrance, and a third story behind an attic parapet.

As completed in 1816, the house had a central hall instead of the oval room on the axis, with a main entrance on the north, no attic or parapet, and a modest stairway on the east side of the entrance.

The unique feature of the house is its domed circular portico, two stories high, on the south front. Half of the "temple" is a semicircular colonnade on the outside, while the other half has a triple French window recessed into the central hall. The pattern has never been duplicated.

Great windows, crowned with arches, set with wide panes and decorated with white stone trim, flank the portico and attest to Thornton's flair for handling details, as do the flat treatment of the cornice, the delicate, classic moldings, and the gracefully turned balustrades.

Less elaborate, almost stark by contrast, is the main entrance, the north facade, presenting unadorned windows and a doorway with an untrimmed arch and an unpretentious fan transom. But it surveys a splendid circular carriage driveway and a flower garden planted with the finest of box. The east driveway entrance to the estate has a massive iron gate near the wing that was once a stable and coach house.

The entrance of the house opens into a transverse hall, which connects the wings and leads to the main hall, with the drawing room on the left and a conservatory and a study to the east of it. To the right of the hall is a living room, adjoining the stepdown dining room, which was used as a bedroom when the west wing was the residence.

In the east wing is the room that was the medical office of the present owner's grandfather, Dr. Armistead Peter. His mother-in-law installed gas fixtures in the house, but most of the effects remain unchanged. Still there today are the original marble mantels, friezes, wide plank flooring, and sliding doors of polished curly maple with massive brass locks, along with

The great hall, showing the temple portico recessed into the interior with triple French windows.

The parlor, with a
marble mantel, frieze,
and wide-plank floor.

Opposite, and above
Oriental effects combine
with Americana in the
study in the east wing.

sofas, tables, chairs, and cabinets in classic Queen Anne, Regency, Hepple-white, Chippendale, and Sheraton designs.

The house contains a priceless collection of Washington family memo-rabilia.

With the exception of these treasured addenda and modern plumbing, the mansion is virtually unchanged from what it was in the days when Mr. and Mrs. Thomas Peter entertained at a series of brilliant events in its spacious interior.

Thomas Peter was a man of many interests. One was the Washington Jockey Club, which sponsored at the Meridian Hill Track a semiannual series of races for which he officiated as steward. Thornton, also a horse lover, was a member of the club. Colonel John Tayloe was president, and he and his wife often visited Tudor Place. Mrs. Thornton, the former Anna Maria Brodeau of Philadelphia, was an accomplished artist who had studied under Gilbert Stuart, and who spent many of her afternoons with her intimate friend Patty Peter at Tudor Place, while their husbands were with Colonel Tayloe at the races.

Josiah Quincy, a staunch Federalist who was a member of Congress (1805–1813), and his wife were back home in Massachusetts while the Peter home was being built; but letters from Mrs. Peter to Mrs. Quincy indicated that both families had belonged to a tight little group in which friendships were based on mutual disapproval of the Republican (Jefferson and Madison) policies of the day. The exchange of letters also indicated that both women, with strong minds of their own, had a keen interest in public affairs and a devotion to the British Crown right up to the moment war was declared.

In a missive to Mrs. Quincy in 1812, Mrs. Peter lamented the departure of their friend, Sir Augustus John Foster, the British Minister, and added, "It is delightful to meet with those who think and talk as we do. I am resolved to express my sentiments till the sedition law is put in force, and there is not much danger of that until after the next election. Provided the present party, which Heaven forbid, is re-elected, I believe the first law they pass will be that."

At the Peters' house less than two years later, when the family was still living in the west wing before the mansion was finished, Patty Peter and Maria Thornton sat at a bedroom window and watched in horror as smoke and flames enveloped the Capitol and the White House. The next morning, all Georgetown learned that the Navy Yard buildings and the Department headquarters had also been burned, and that Colonel Tayloe had offered The Octagon, just vacated by the French Minister, to Dolley and James Madison for use as their official residence.

Patty Peter's letters to Mrs. Quincy took on a different tone after that. They were full of pity for the American troops and resentment for the now-recognized enemy. The last vestige of local sympathy toward the British had, literally, gone up in smoke, and Federalists loyally joined forces with Republicans for the duration.

By the time the Peters' mansion was finished, the war was over; but resentment against George IV of the House of Hanover still ran high. This may have been one reason that Thornton's masterpiece soon came to be known as Tudor Place—a kind of defiance to the hated name of Hanover. More than likely, however, the house was so named because it fitted in with the owner's initials—T.P.

In any event, Tudor Place soon became famous as the setting for brilliant social events and the focal attraction for celebrated visitors from all over the country and abroad. Lafayette was entertained there on his last trip to America in 1824, and he was accompanied by a dashing aide, Captain Williams, who fell in love with a pretty daughter of the household, America Peter, and later married her.

General Robert E. Lee and his wife, a niece of Mrs. Peter, were frequent callers at Tudor Place, and the general's visit there in 1869, shortly after the defeat of the Confederacy, was widely publicized.

In addition to their three patriotically named daughters—America, Columbia, and Britannia Wellington—Thomas and Martha Peter had five other children. After Thomas Peter died in 1834, his widow lived on at Tudor Place for a number of years. Meanwhile, Britannia, who married Commodore Beverly Kennon, was widowed before she was thirty when her husband was killed by an explosion of the USS *Princeton* in 1844. With her infant daughter, Martha Custis Kennon, she returned to live with Mrs. Peter, who was dividing her time between Tudor Place and her country home, near Seneca, Maryland.

Britannia, who inherited Tudor Place in 1854 (when her mother died, having, according to the will, "long survived her husband and her other children having received their inheritance"), lived there most of her remaining years.

For a brief period, shortly before the Civil War, however, she leased the house to a Virginia gentleman named Pendleton. He hurriedly left Washington after Virginia seceded from the Union; and when Mrs. Kennon learned that the United States government was on the verge of commandeering Tudor Place for use as a hospital, she rushed back and announced that she would occupy and open it to Federal officers for living quarters "on condition that affairs of war should not be discussed" in her presence. Then, before her new boarders had a chance to move in, she carefully stored away the precious Washington relics she had inherited and most of her other choice possessions.

After the war, she resumed her gracious way of life and her activity in social and civic affairs, and placed on display the memorabilia, which many visitors wanted to see. They were particularly interested in the miniatures and in Martha Washington's lavender wedding slippers.

Sarah Washburn Tiffey, who in 1869 went to work for the Mount Vernon Ladies' Association, and was of tremendous help to Ann Pamela Cunningham in preserving the estate, kept a diary that includes a reference to Britannia Kennon. The 1870 entry had to do with a visit that Mrs. Tiffey and Miss Cunningham made to Washington to hear a lecture by Benson

Lossing and to see the Senate Sergeant-at-Arms on Capitol Hill. "He took us to a lunchroom where we had stewed oysters, cold turkey, tea, etc.," wrote Mrs. Tiffey, "and he gave us his carriage from one to six. We went to Georgetown to see Mrs. Kennon, where we were beautifully received, treated to cake and wine, and shown most of the exquisite miniatures of General and Mrs. Washington, and many interesting relics. Nothing could exceed the sweetness of Mrs. Kennon, and we were cordially invited again."

A stranger, who shortly after that asked permission to see the miniatures, was graciously received by Mrs. Kennon and described her as "very tall, very slender, with the figure and grace of a young woman." The caller also mentioned "the generous manner with which she took great pains" to conduct the visitor on a tour of the mansion.

When Mrs. Kennon died in 1911 at the age of ninety-six, her obituary in the Baltimore *Sun* praised her as "the centre of an intellectual and cultural society," recalled her as being "always in touch with the progress of events in the world," and mentioned that she was the first president of the National Society of Colonial Dames in the District of Columbia and among the earlier presidents of the Louise Home, a residence founded by W. W. Corcoran for indigent, aged gentlewomen of southern birth.

Mrs. Kennon's only child, Martha, whose death preceded that of her mother by a number of years, had married a distant cousin, Dr. Armistead Peter, who inherited the estate and restored its original name. An active practicing physician for many years, Dr. Peter died at Tudor Place in 1902, leaving the estate to his son, Armistead Peter, Jr., who died there in 1960.

Armistead Peter III, who presides over the stately mansion today, is a widower, artist, and writer, who is now completing a definitive history of Tudor Place. Meanwhile, he has taken some decisive steps toward preserving the property.

Although Tudor Place was declared a national landmark in 1960, Mr. Peter was not content to rely on that citation to protect the historic estate that has been in his family for more than one hundred and sixty years. He was well aware that other properties similarly designated had later been demolished or drastically altered. He searched avidly for some additional safeguard, and found it—in the 1936 Historic Sites Act. And in 1966, he became the first individual to make use of this law by donating to the Secretary of the Interior the scenic easement to Tudor Place.

This does not mean that he gave the government the mansion or the land, but rather that he granted Uncle Sam the right and privilege of protecting Tudor Place, exactly as it is now, from realty encroachments. Specifically, the scenic easement provides that the estate cannot be subdivided or redeveloped, and that the house can only be used as a private residence or a museum.

Now under the pledged protection of the government, the grand old mansion is destined to remain much the same as it has been since 1816—a splendid example of uncluttered Americana at its architectural best. Mr. Peter, meanwhile, has provided for the permanent support of the house and grounds after his death.

Original furnishings and family memorabilia in the living room.

The dining room, adjoining the living room.

VII

FIRENZE HOUSE

A haven for priceless paneling, English and French antiques, an extraordinary glass collection, and valuable paintings is Firenze House, the residence of Mr. and Mrs. John A. Logan, with two addresses—2800 Albemarle Street and 4400 Broad Branch Road.

Set in twenty-two rolling acres on the edge of Rock Creek Park, the Tudor structure is of gray fieldstone, quarried on the estate and relieved with a mellowing limestone trim. Dormers with diamond-shaped panes, bay windows, a complex gable roof of variegated slate, and shallow moldings are some of the architectural distinctions of this baronial mansion, which has green shutters and awnings to match.

The three stories and basement house fifty-nine rooms, including baths; and the estate has several other buildings with sizable living quarters. The gatehouse at the Broad Branch Road entrance has five rooms and two baths; the nearby garage, a six-room apartment over it; and Mrs. Logan's art studio, a big room and a bath with storage areas below.

A formal rose garden, in which tulips and dahlias also bloom in season, replaced the tennis courts on one side of the main house some years ago. Lordly stone lions survey the magnificent woodland scene from a brick terrace on another side. An estimated total of ten thousand trees, many of them dogwood, and three-hundred-year-old box burgeon on this "country estate" within the District of Columbia; and the driveway from Broad Branch Road passes a ninety-foot-long swimming pool, which was put in before the house was built.

The interior is eclectic, incorporating effects of a number of influences and eras. No attempt has been made to recapture the atmosphere of any one period, and yet there is no abrupt transition from one to another. Varied components, ranging all the way from the Charles II table in the center of the dining room to the modern bowling alley in the basement, are beautifully integrated. The elegant Georgian drawing room, Adam dining room, French powder room, and great hall with a cantilevered balcony and a massive, carved oak stairway are among the many parts compatibly juxta-

View of Firenze House from the terrace side, overlooking Rock Creek Park.

posed in this Tudor house with an Italian name, Georgian and Adam touches, and a predominance of Louis XV and XVI furnishings.

The original owner of the house was Blanche Estabrook (Mrs. Arthur) O'Brien, widow of Paul Roebling, a member of the Trenton, New Jersey, family noted for executing the Brooklyn Bridge. She was the wife of Colonel O'Brien when the house was begun in 1925, with Russell O. Kluge as architect and H. F. Huber as interior designer. The coordinator of construction was retired General Richard Marshall, formerly of the Army Engineers Corps.

Completed in 1927 and named Estabrook, the house was the scene of a number of memorable events, including the 1929 debut of Mrs. O'Brien's daughter Caroline, and the latter's marriage to Alexander Hagner the following June.

In the 1930's, the property was leased to the Minister of Hungary and Mme. John Pelenyi, who made it a popular gathering place for diplomats, high officials, and residential notables until 1940. Then Pelenyi broke with his government, resigned as envoy, and moved away from Washington. His successor as Hungarian Minister, George de Ghika, and his daughter lived quietly at Estabrook until it was sold in 1941.

Driveway entrance to the house.

The buyers were Colonel and Mrs. M. Robert Guggenheim, who were residing on their oceangoing yacht, *Firenze,* when the United States Navy requested it for wartime service. One of Colonel Guggenheim's favorite possessions, the *Firenze* had been christened with the Italian equivalent of Florence, the name of his mother who was devoted to things Italian; but he turned the vessel over to the government at once. Then he purchased Estabrook and promptly renamed it—Firenze House.

The Guggenheim millions, along with experts in architecture and interior designing, and the exceptional taste and prior possessions of the new owners contributed toward making the mansion what it is today. Comparatively few changes were imposed on the façade, but, although none of the rooms was altered as to size, the atmosphere of the interior was completely transformed.

Like many great houses built in the 1920's, this one originally had a somber setting to augment heavy Jacobean furnishings. The new owners wanted a lighter effect, so as the first of many alterations they had the dark woodwork in the great hall pickled a pale gray. The beamed-effect ceiling in the drawing room, reputed to be more than two hundred years old and to have once adorned a sailing ship, was removed. The operation posed fewer problems than were anticipated, for workmen soon discovered that the covering was not beamed at all; the appearance had been achieved by tacking wide boards together and attaching them to the ceiling.

The soft blue-gray walls of the Georgian drawing room as they are today resulted from painstaking care on the part of Mrs. Logan, then Mrs. Guggenheim. A trained artist with a keen perception of color, she mixed the paint herself, and came up with seventeen shades before she got the one she wanted.

Marble mantel in the drawing room, with portrait above of Mrs. Logan framed by Grinling Gibbons' carving.

Decorated with a lavish touch, the room has exquisite paneling, im-

ported from England, and a teakwood floor. Grinling Gibbons' carved swags, romantic figures, wreaths, and garlands adorn the walls and are elaborately patterned over the Sir Christopher Wren marble mantel. Two enormous Waterford crystal chandeliers and matching sconces are in this salon; also, a palace-sized Kerman carpet, Louis XVI sofas and chairs, marquetry tables, and two long Chinese mirrors with lacquered frames, from the Halifax estate in England.

On either side of the doorway leading to the screened sun porch, shelved cases before the broad windows display the late Colonel Guggenheim's glass collection. Included are compotes and decanters of cut crystal, goblets with cased bowls, wine glasses engraved with chinoiserie subjects, delicate pastel vases and bottles, and ale glasses with faceted stems. Colonel Guggenheim was particularly interested in American glass and fascinated with the creations of the German-born designer Steigel, who did much of his work in this country; there are many Steigel masterpieces in the assemblage, which also includes representative items from seventeenth-, eighteenth-, and nineteenth-century France and England.

Van Dyck's "Earl of Arundel," with the sixteenth-century medallion and pendant pictured in the portrait, and Murillo's "Salvatori Mundi," the two most valuable paintings in Firenze House, are also in this room.

The great hall, with its walls three stories high and its beamed ceiling, underwent several drastic changes under the Guggenheims' direction. The organ's gilt pipes, which had contrasted nicely with the original dark walls and carved staircase, were toned to silver to blend with the newly pickled woodwork, and then partially concealed by the minstrel gallery. Gold and cream brocade curtains were hung to enhance the mullioned windows that emphasize the Tudor style of the house. Comfortable chairs and sofas were arranged near the enormous fireplace that dominates one side of the room. A rare Queen Anne table of English elm is an especially fine piece here, and another is the William and Mary corner cupboard, which displays Mr. Logan's notable Dresden collection.

A unique feature of the house is the little rotunda between the drawing room and the great hall, its ceiling highlighted by bas-relief signs of the zodiac, and its floor centered with a compass designed in rare wood and embellished with brass points.

To the left of the great hall is the Adam dining room, so called for its Adam mantel and lighted cabinets in the Adam tradition. The walls are paneled, providing a warm background for the Charles II dining table of burled walnut trimmed with Brazilian tulipwood, a rich eighteenth-century Khorassan rug in the Herati design, and antique sideboards. Every piece in the room is an antique, in fact, except the twenty-six Queen Anne chairs, which are reproductions, upholstered in rose velvet to blend with the Venetian velvet curtains.

Over the mantel is Jacomo Victor's "Barnyard Scene," dated 1672. A choice collection of Georgian silver is on the Hepplewhite sideboard, and a pair of Queen Anne mirrors are among other pieces of museum status in this room.

Window shelves displaying the extraordinary glass collection in the drawing room.

85

THE EARL OF ARUNDEL
FORMERLY IN THE ORLEANS GALLERY
VAN DYCK

27

The library, with
paneling by Sir
Christopher Wren.

Van Dyck's portrait of
the Earl of Arundel in
the drawing room.

The library to the left of the main entrance is a constructional gem,
with paneling by Sir Christopher Wren, who made it for his own study in
London. Grinling Gibbons' carvings of a grouse and a duck further decorate
the room, in which there is also an interesting collection of glass paper-
weights.

The master bedroom, sitting room, and guest suites on the second floor
are reached by the central stairway and an elevator. Bedrooms for servants
are on the third floor, and additional rooms for the staff are over the kitchen
and pantry area.

Among the noteworthy items in the house is the one to the right of the
main entrance—a canopied coachman's chair from an eighteenth-century
English castle. It stands near the doorway to the powder room, which has
pale green doors and window frames from France, Louis XV chairs, a sofa
upholstered in original Beauvais tapestry, a handsome Louis XVI desk, and a
dainty French dressing table.

The minstrel gallery in the great hall.

The little rotunda, between the great hall and the drawing room.

The great hall, showing
the carved staircase.

Few homes lend themselves to entertaining more gracefully than does
Firenze House, and it has long been one of the city's most active social
locales, with formal dinners for twenty-six guests, receptions for from five to
six hundred, and garden parties for up to a thousand as annual highlights of
the Capital calendar. Particularly brilliant some years ago were the Christmas parties, with the great hall decked with holly, pine, and red satin
garlands, and guests singing carols while pipe organ music resounded
through the palatial dwelling.

Two Titian portraits and much of the inestimable paneling were
destroyed in a three-alarm fire that swept through the mansion while the
owners were away in the winter of 1946. Michael Rosenaur was immediately
engaged to restore the interior, and by the end of the year Firenze House was
again a showplace and social focus of Washington.

The Adam dining
room.

Choice assemblage of
Georgian silver,
displayed on the
Hepplewhite sideboard
in the dining room.

90

VIII

FOREIGN SPLENDOR

Ambassadorial mansions abound in the nation's Capital, but several, having been built specifically for that purpose and with no local historic connection, might well be considered great houses *in* but not *of* Washington. As an example, the British Ambassador's red brick residence at 3100 Massachusetts Avenue, designed in 1930 by Sir Edwin Lutyens as a manor house in the Queen Anne tradition, has no indigenous ties to Washington and symbolizes Britain at its sedate best. Similarly, the contemporary white stucco edifice at 2443 Massachusetts Avenue, erected in 1929 by the government of Venezuela, is patently an architectural entity of that country, rather than of Washington. In the same category is the Renaissance villa erected by the Italian government in the late 1920's at 2700 Sixteenth Street.

Other splendid houses, which from their inception have been properties of foreign nations, include the neoclassic Japanese Embassy at 2514 Massachusetts Avenue, the ultramodern Danish Embassy at 3200 Whitehaven Street, and the fabulous Middle-Eastern complex that is the Embassy of Kuwait at 2940 Tilden Street. A number of envoys reside in imposing houses purchased by their governments from Washington residents, but comparatively few such houses are great, either from an architectural standpoint or because of their association with distinguished Americans.

The French Ambassador's Residence

Among those diplomatic mansions that meet both standards of greatness is the residence of the French Ambassador at 2221 Kalorama Road. Called "the most embassy-like of all embassies in Washington," this property had an illustrious connection with Washington history for a quarter of a century before it was purchased by the French government.

Set back from the street in a grove of trees, it is a neo-Tudor stone and brick structure with spreading wings, which give it a wide front on Kalorama Road. From the flagstone terrace and rolling gardens to the rear, it com-

mands one of the most famous views of Washington—the picturesque Taft Bridge above the towering trees of Rock Creek Park. The estate covers slightly less than four acres. The house has thirty-four rooms on four floors, including the basement, and a collection of tastefully selected furnishings, of which many pieces recall highlights of the mansion's history.

Built by one wealthy American and owned for many years by another, the dwelling was internationally known for the constant stream of royal and other personages who were entertained there over a span of twenty years.

The late Henri de Sibour designed the house for William W. Lawrence, a tycoon in white lead interests. Completed in 1910, it was sold shortly thereafter to John Hays Hammond, the multimillionaire gold and diamond mining engineer, whose spectacular career extended from the California gold fields, railroads of the West, and irrigation projects in Mexico to the South African Transvaal.

By the time Hammond decided to settle in Washington, he had become active in the field of social welfare and political thought, and was a close friend of several government leaders. When President William Howard Taft in 1911 named him special ambassador to the coronation of King George V, it was the first of several of his official appointments that were internationally prestigious. He was president of the Panama Pacific Exposition to Europe in 1912; chairman of the World Court Commission, 1914–1915; and chairman of the United States Coal Commission, 1922–1923. During these years and later, he and Mrs. Hammond entertained virtually every celebrated figure who visited Washington from abroad. Their house was also the scene of many parties for the younger set, centering around their daughter, Natalie Hays Hammond, who was a Capital belle, and their son, John Hays Hammond, Jr., who was graduated from Sheffield Engineering School at Yale in 1910, and was to become famous in his own right as an inventor of a system of selective radio telegraphy, an improvement for pipe organ mechanisms, and a new type of modulator for the piano.

Mrs. Hammond died in 1921, and three months later, her husband, son, and daughter left Washington, never again to occupy the house of Kalorama Road. From then until his death in 1936 at the age of eighty-one, John Hays Hammond divided his time between his summer home in Gloucester, Massachusetts, and his winter home in Boca Raton, Florida, visiting Washington only occasionally to look after his Kalorama Road property. Several foreign governments had been interested in it for some time, and the Brazilian government twice had tried to negotiate a purchase, but Mr. Hammond sold the house to the French Republic a month before he died. With it went the furnishings, much to the delight of the new occupants, the French Ambassador André de Laboulaye and his family.

The edifice inside was an elegant museum piece of its era, with heavily carved woodwork and a treasure trove of Empire sofas from France, ornate marble-topped tables from Italy, and a sofa and six chairs from Russia. The handsome rug in the main sitting room was woven to Mrs. Hammond's express order in Madrid, and the paintings and art objects from all over the world might well have been selected for a foreign ambassador's residence.

Mme. de Laboulaye, presiding over France's first permanent home in Washington, made few major changes in the interior, but Sèvres china, Baccarat glass, Porthault linens, and exquisite silver embossed with "R.F." (*République Française*) were supplied by the Mobilier National, the national storehouse of furnishings, to give a French flavor to the house. At the same time, extensive work was done on the grounds. Shrubs and hedges and a profusion of flowers were planted in the gardens and around the house itself.

The characteristically French atmosphere of the residence today has been achieved by several of Mme. de Laboulaye's successors, although World

View of the French Ambassador's residence from Kalorama Road.

The main hallway.

The Empire drawing room.

War II halted all decorative projects for a time. On June 25, 1940, the tricolor at the embassy entrance was placed at half mast as France officially laid down her arms. Not long afterward, the Vichy government's Ambassador Gaston Henry-Haye arrived to replace the popular Count René Doynel de St. Quentin, and to inherit his superb wine cellar and chef. Both of these envoys were bachelors who entertained purposefully and constantly, but neither one had the time or inclination to have worn furnishings repaired or to order new ones.

After the United States broke relations with the Vichy government in November, 1942, the French Embassy was placed under guardianship of the Swiss Legation, and the residence was unoccupied for almost two years. Henri Etienne Hoppenot, De Gaulle's special delegate to the United States, presided over the reopening on September 24, 1944, and in December, Ambassador Henri Bonnet, representing the French Provisional government, arrived in Washington. Mme. Bonnet at once took over redecorating chores. She rearranged much of the furniture, had some of it reupholstered, and ordered a magnificent crystal chandelier for the Empire drawing room. She also enclosed the loggia on the west, and made it a charming sunroom, now called the *salon gris* (gray salon) .

Mme. Couve de Murville, the next ambassador's wife, acquired comfortable sofas and chairs for the sitting room, had a Napoleonic table copied to make a pair for the Empire drawing room, and replaced some of the rugs. Her immediate successor, the first Mme. Alphand, refurbished the sunroom, with stark white and black accents relieved by touches of gray and green; but her most memorable contribution to the decor was the use of artificial flowers interlaced with fresh blossoms in massive and beautifully deceptive arrangements. Such bouquets are seen all over the French Embassy today, and also in many other Washington houses.

Nicole Alphand, the second wife of Ambassador Hervé Alphand, redecorated the house from attic to basement during her seven years in Washington. Under her aegis, the dark interior was perceptibly lightened, and the French atmosphere was enhanced by the addition of seventeenth-century paintings in the dining room, abstract and impressionist pictures in the Empire drawing room, new upholstery and draperies throughout the house, and the replacement of several carpets.

Mme. Lucet, the current chatelaine, said she had no plans for major decorative changes when her husband became ambassador in 1967; but a notable piece that she ordered for the *salon de bois* (wood room) is now a distinctive addition. It is an eighteenth-century walnut desk with a beautiful sheen, simple lines, and ormolu mounts.

The charm of the mansion is apparent from the moment one enters the main hallway, which leads to the dining room on the right, the Empire drawing room on the left, and the *salon de bois,* which opens onto the terrace at the rear. The hallway has an elaborately molded ceiling and a grand stairway with an intricately carved rail, which was once dark but later pickled to a soft gray-beige tone. The latter blends nicely with the cream plastering that replaced the original dark paneled walls. Over the

Gray and green combined with black and white accent the sunroom—the *salon gris.*

The *salon du bois.*

staircase a tapestry, patterned after a seventeenth-century painting, romantically symbolizes Africa. A Louis XV sofa, upholstered in beige and crimson fabric, is at the base of the staircase; and to the left of the entrance, a marble-topped seventeenth-century Italian table displays an enormous bouquet of flowers before a tall mirror with an elaborate gilt frame. Other select items in the hallway include three Gobelin rugs, a Louis XV marble-topped console below a seventeenth-century painted panel of the same style as those on the dining-room walls, and a reproduction of a Houdon bust of Lafayette, which was presented to the embassy by Messmore Kendall, president of the Society of American Friends of Lafayette, in November, 1953.

The Empire drawing room blends Empire chairs, sofas, and tables with Sèvres ashtrays, bisque shepherdesses and cupids; and couples contemporary French paintings against an off-white background with a red Ionic key motif on the draperies, the cornice, and some of the upholstery. Most of the basic furniture in this room was purchased with the house, but the two Napoleonic tables and the twin blue love seats that flank the fireplace were added later, along with several other charming effects. The 160-year-old Aubusson rug plays a soft red pattern against a beige and gray background. Two Empire armchairs upholstered in emerald velvet contrast nicely with pastels in the decor. A Matisse painting, yellow and blue predominating, hangs to the right of the Empire marble mantelpiece; a Bonnard still life is over the sofa on the opposite side of the room. The enormous crystal chandelier, wall brackets, and a pair of tall lamps with elaborate gold leaf bases are other exceptional furnishings here.

Off the Empire drawing room is the *salon gris,* a cozy retreat with gray brick walls and a cream tile ceiling, and gray accents combined with black and white. Against the wall directly across from the baronial fireplace, a big sofa, upholstered in black velvet, has gray pillows. Sofas on either side of the mantel are covered in gray fabric, set off with green pillows. The occasional tables are of black lacquer banded with brass, on which rest alabaster glasses for cigarettes. The curtains are gray silk twill. A grand piano fills a corner, and, across the room, a round table has a cover of pale green and white damask to match the two overstuffed chairs on either side. The modern rug with its geometric black design woven on a white background gives a chiaroscuro effect.

Because of its elaborate paneling, the sitting room that centers the rear of the house is called the *salon de bois.* The original twenty-foot ceiling was lowered to give a better proportion to the whole. An oriental rug in tones of orange, beige, green, and blue warms the room. The tailored hangings combine dove-gray curtains with beige overdraperies that match the cornice. Three sofas and easy chairs, upholstered in blond velvet, and a stone-carved mantelpiece are used in the room; a round table with a down-to-the-floor cover—something of a decorative signature in the embassy—is done here in larkspur-blue fabric.

Walls of the dining room are dramatized with vivid green paneling, classic pilasters defined with gilt, and seven seventeenth-century paintings of fanciful figures. The set, restored by Boudin of Paris, once adorned the Petit

Fanciful figures in paintings from Versailles, green paneling, and classic gilt pilasters brighten the dining room.

Trianon and is on loan from Versailles. The ceiling-high antique mirror over the Empire mantel is centered with a Louis XIV clock, and the carpet is a soft patterned green square with a wide beige border.

Master bedrooms and guest suites—nine large rooms in all—are on the second floor; the staff occupies ten rooms on the third. The kitchen and pantries are on the basement floor, as is a refrigerated room for meats and perishable vegetables and fruit. A dumbwaiter from the kitchen to the butler's pantry off the dining room is electrically propelled.

A three-alarm fire in May, 1961, threatened to demolish the house. Flames destroyed a third of the roof, impaired the ceiling in the main salon and the walls of the second and third floors, while smoke and fire almost ruined some of the carpets and curtains in the west wing. But most of the valuable effects were miraculously saved; and within six months the mansion was restored to an excellent showcase for France as well as a comfortable domicile for her top diplomatic representative in the United States.

The Brazilian Ambassador's Residence

Constructed the same year as the French Embassy and enhanced with an equally distinguished Washington history, the Brazilian Ambassador's official residence in Washington is at 3000 Massachusetts Avenue.

The original owner was Robert Sanderson McCormick, diplomat and world traveler, who built the house for his wife, Katherine van Etta Medill McCormick, daughter of the Chicago publisher, Joseph Medill. John Russell Pope designed the house in early Renaissance style, with a recessed entrance derived from Peruzzi's Palazzo Massimi Colonne in Rome.

Mr. and Mrs. McCormick's two sons—Robert R., who was to become publisher of the Chicago *Tribune,* and Medill, who was to be a United States senator—were young men in 1902 when their father was appointed the first American Ambassador to Austria-Hungary. Subsequently, he served for two years as Ambassador to Russia, and two more as Ambassador to France.

In 1909, he employed Pope to design a house in the palazzo tradition, which would be an appropriate setting for the collection of furnishings, art objects, and curios that he and his wife had acquired on his tours of duty abroad and in their world travels.

They had a remarkable assemblage of Empire sofas and chairs, Italian consoles and chests, Aubusson rugs, and magnificent crystal chandeliers, all of which were beautifully intermingled in the classic house with its marble and Caen stone accents. In such a background of grandeur, Mr. and Mrs. McCormick entertained notables continually.

McCormick died in 1919. Not long afterward, when Medill McCormick died, his mother gave the mansion to his widow, Ruth Hanna McCormick. She later married Albert G. Simms, and was prominent in the socio-political set of Washington for several years. In 1934, the mansion caught the fancy of the Brazilian Ambassador Oswaldo Aranha, and he persuaded his government to buy it and much of its furnishings.

One of Aranha's successors, Ambassador Mauricio Nabuco, said of the embassy residence, "Outside it is Italian; inside it is Portuguese, French, and English." By the time he was assigned to Washington in 1948, several

View of the façade of the Brazilian Ambassador's residence, with its recessed entrance in the palazzo tradition.

Acme of Old World
splendor is the main
salon, the original
ballroom of the
mansion.

The dining room, with
scenes on the
nineteenth-century
wallpaper depicting
Portugal's great colony
in the New World.

striking touches recalled the impact of Portugal on what was once its greatest colony. Nabuco added authentic Brazilian accents, reflecting Portuguese influence. Prior to the 1949 visit of Brazil's President Eurico Gaspar Dutra, Nabuco had the mansion redecorated in part, and it was then that the early nineteenth-century mural wallpaper in the dining room, depicting scenes after drawings by Johann Rugendas, was installed. A German artist who visited Brazil in 1800, Rugendas was enchanted with the vast and verdant panorama of the Portuguese stronghold in the New World. To make the wallpaper, his paintings were copied and printed from the original blocks by Zuber of Alsace. It is as old as the wallpaper of American scenes in the diplomatic reception room in the White House. The colors are remarkably clear, the figures and the lush landscape sharply defined.

Three handsome rosewood chests in the entrance hall of the embassy and the eighteenth-century solid silver chandelier are from an old vestry in the state of Minas Gerais. Dominating the hallway is the grand marble staircase, with balusters of hand-carved rosewood, and an intricate wrought-iron rail, sweeping upward in a graceful curve.

A ballroom, which is almost as big as a tennis court, a drawing room, and a sitting room are on the second floor. The ballroom is lavish with gold leaf details on the walls and ceiling. Its marvelous mirrors reflect the Old World splendor of Empire furniture upholstered in rose and beige petit point, the largest and finest rose and beige Aubusson rug in Washington, and art objects from France, England, Italy, Portugal, and Brazil.

For some years, a featured portrait in the main sitting room was that of José Sylvestre Rebello, first Brazilian envoy to the United States, painted in 1826 by an American, Sarah M. Peale. But a recent ambassador, Vasco Leitao de Cunha, had it removed to his chancery office, and replaced it with a work by a contemporary Brazilian artist, which is in keeping with other modern paintings that have been added to the house in recent years.

A patio and gardens are on one side of the house. The other side is closed off from Massachusetts Avenue by tall evergreens, and the front faces a long lawn and a driveway winding in from the street.

Containing some of the finest European antiques in Washington, as well as excellent pieces in rosewood and jacaranda from Brazil, a rare collection of colonial silver, and the beautiful nineteenth-century wallpaper, the Brazilian Embassy residence is, indeed, a great house of Washington.

The drawing room, adjoining the main salon.

The large sitting room, with contemporary furniture and modern Brazilian paintings.

The Spanish Embassy

The Spanish Embassy at 2801 Sixteenth Street gracefully bridges the gap between being a great house in, rather than of, Washington. Though built by an American, it was never occupied by anyone except successive Spanish envoys and their families. The compound today includes both the ambassador's residence and the chancery, which has its entrance on Fifteenth Street.

Completed in 1923, the house was built by Mrs. John B. Henderson, wife of a onetime senator from Missouri. An eccentric who dabbled heavily in real estate, she bought more than a hundred lots on upper Sixteenth Street with the hope of making that area the elite residential section of Washington.

George Oakley Totten was the architect for this mansion, designed in white stone after a Venetian palace. Mrs. Henderson offered it to the United States government for use as the official home of the Vice President. Calvin Coolidge, who held that post when the house was finished, had several times suggested publicly that the government should provide a Vice Presidential residence and sufficient funds to maintain it. But he was not tempted by Mrs. Henderson's proposition. "A hotel is sufficient for my needs," he said, and continued living at The Willard. But the real reason for his refusal was that Congress failed to act on the offer, and he felt that the house was too grand for him to maintain.

The Spanish government bought it in 1926, and shortly thereafter, the interior began to show marked Spanish influences. When the adjoining chancery was built, the patio tiles were brought from Seville and Valencia, and the wrought-iron doors and grilles from Toledo.

Successive envoys and their wives incorporated other authentic Spanish touches, sometimes using their personal possessions. The house has progressively taken on the character of the country to which it belongs, and, particularly in recent years, it has become the epitome of Spanish elegance.

The exterior of Spain's official mansion in Washington.

Dramatic redecoration of the house was carried out in 1965 by the current ambassador's wife, the Marquesa de Merry del Val, who with her husband arrived the previous year and at once launched plans to make the superbly appointed but impersonal embassy into an equally impressive but more warmly inviting home.

Working with Duarte d'Avilla Pinto Coelho, her favorite Madrid interior designer, she transformed the ballroom into an intimate salon ("our American friends call it the red salon," she said recently). The result is a charming room, with walls of crimson flocked silk, and chairs and divans upholstered in damask and velvet in shades ranging from cerise to deep ruby, to accentuate the muted colors of two large seventeenth-century Flemish tapestries woven by Jan Raes. The four chandeliers are from the famous crystal factory in La Granja, Segovia. These, like most of the finer furnishings, were sent to the embassy by the Fundación Generalísimo Franco in Madrid, but the marquesa acquired the red salon's two-hundred-year-old Persian rug in New York.

Two sizable sitting rooms, the yellow salon and the white salon, have rich carpets woven in Spain. A portrait attributed to Goya, believed to be a study of the famous actress Tirana, attracts special attention in the yellow salon, as do two French-style pastel portraits of the daughters of Philip V by Van Loo, and two sketches by Eugénio Lucas, Goya's celebrated follower. A silver urn presented to the ambassador's father by the Duke of Alba is also in the yellow salon; and around the base of the urn is an amber rosary that belonged to the ambassador's uncle, the late Cardinal Merry del Val, a noted Vatican Secretary of State.

The white salon shelters an exceptional eighteenth-century tapestry, woven by Teniers for the Royal Palace in Madrid. The Mengs portrait of Charles III was owned by the Spanish mission to the United States in 1781, and above the eighteenth-century mantel, the visage of Baron de Carondolet, first Spanish Governor of Louisiana and West Florida, solemnly surveys the room.

The patio.

Also adorning the ballroom and salons are personal possessions of the Ambassador and the Marquesa de Merry del Val, several of which were acquired when he was envoy to Peru, just before coming to Washington. Archangels of the Peruvian colonial period appear serenely at home on either side of an Empire fireplace and Queen Isabel de Farnesio's portrait by an unknown artist of the Castilian school. On a table in the ballroom is a collection of silver *zapatillas* (Peruvian stirrups for women horseback riders), along with silver ashtrays and fighting cocks, which the marquesa crafted by her own design in Lima.

Among many other unusual items in the residence is the mosaic of Our Lady of Los Reyes, patroness of Seville, between two Toledo wrought-iron lamps in the patio; and above the door leading to the chancery is a painting of Charles III's coat of arms, which links Spanish and American history. The emblem once belonged to Don Diego Gardoqui, first Spanish envoy sent to the United States, who became a close personal friend of President Washington. Copies of correspondence between the two are on display in the patio.

The ballroom,
transformed into an
intimate salon.

The first effects, which impress guests on arrival at the embassy and are glimpsed with renewed appreciation as they leave, are in the main entrance hall. They include religious paintings from colonial Peru, two royal Spanish portraits from the Prado Museum by the eighteenth-century French artist J. Ranc, and Leon Leoni's marble bust of Charles V.

A superbly appointed mansion of which any nation would be proud, this residence inspired the late Alben W. Barkley to express the feeling of many Americans when, on visiting the Spanish embassy as Vice President, he observed, "I'm rather sorry Uncle Sam didn't see fit to accept Mrs. Henderson's offer in 1923."

Pages 112–113

The yellow salon.   Mosaic portrait of Our
Lady of Los Reyes,
flanked by wrought-iron
lamps, in the tiled
patio.

The Mexican Embassy

One of the biggest embassy complexes in Washington has a glittering background of Capital history and some of the world's most magnificent murals, among such glamorous addenda as a music room that is a replica of one at Fontainebleau, and a conservatory with walls of Puebla decorative tiles. This, the property of the Mexican government, at 2829 Sixteenth Street, is a rectangular, four-story, buff brick mansion with the chancery to the back and side.

The dwelling itself figured prominently in Washington's social annals for a decade before it became a foreign possession. Its story began early in 1911, when the massive residence was being built. Nathan C. Wyeth was known to be the architect, but the owner's identity was a carefully guarded secret until December 24 of that year, when Mrs. Franklin MacVeagh invited her husband to visit the house with her. At the time they were living across and down the street in the Pink Palace (now headquarters of the Inter-American Defense Board), and Mr. MacVeagh was President Taft's Secretary of the Treasury. The new edifice being finished and completely furnished, and Mr. MacVeagh having expressed his admiration of both the exterior and the appointments inside, his wife, so the story goes, presented the house to him as a Christmas present.

Surely, few husbands have ever received a more magnificent gift. In addition to the ornate music room, the dwelling had a sitting room with twenty-four-karat-gold walls, and the largest private dining room in Washington. Such a splendid setting was ideal for the season's most brilliant party, a housewarming that was a reception, ball, and supper in honor of Miss Helen Taft, debutante daughter of the President.

The event made social history on more than one account. President and Mrs. Taft and all members of his Cabinet and their wives attended; so did hundreds of other Capital notables; and nobody was distressed when the electricity failed. Guests had an even gayer time waltzing and two-stepping, and later dining by candlelight.

Mrs. MacVeagh died in 1916, and her husband moved out of the house. During the next five years, he leased it to several distinguished occupants. Breckinridge Long, later to be Franklin Roosevelt's first Ambassador to Italy and then Assistant Secretary of State, and Mrs. Long took it in 1918. The

Residence of the
Mexican Ambassador.

115

Roberto Cueva del Rio's mural, as seen on the second floor. The mural begins in the main hallway and continues to the third floor.

The French Renaissance sitting room.

The music room.

The dining room.

following year the Longs turned it over to King Albert and Queen Elizabeth of Belgium and their son Prince Leopold for use during their visit. England's Prime Minister Balfour also stayed in the house while the Longs were tenants.

When the Mexican government purchased the property in 1921, MacVeagh made two specific requests: That there be no major alterations until after his death, and that his favorite servant have lifetime employment.

Both requests were granted. The Mexican envoy did not move into the house until 1925, and almost no changes in decor and furnishings were made until MacVeagh died in 1934. Even then, the ambassador made it clear that any forthcoming changes would harmonize Mexican effects with those already in the house.

The colorful murals, which began to adorn the mansion in 1934, made a dramatic difference, however. Starting with the lower staircase and covering nine walls all the way to the third floor, the series presents stylized scenes of Mexico, its people in many walks of life, and highlights of its history and folklore. An especially impressive segment symbolizes solidarity of the Western Hemisphere in a giant handclasp, and incorporates portraits of such great heroes as Washington, Hidalgo, Bolívar, Juárez, Lincoln, and Martí. Roberto Cueva del Rio of Mexico City was twenty-three when he started the paintings in 1934. He did not finish them until 1941.

Elsewhere in the residence other Mexican effects have been beautifully blended into the original setting. In the entrance hall is an eighteenth-century wood altarpiece with four mirrors and sculptured religious figures, and a broad stairway with an elaborately hand-carved balustrade.

On the second floor the grand music room is very much as it was originally. At one end a pipe organ graces a small stage, while a majestic fireplace dominates the opposite end. A Palladian window opens from the salon to a small balcony over the main entrance porte cochere.

Adjoining the music room is the French Renaissance sitting room. The twenty-four-karat-gold wallpaper has long since been replaced by oyster brocade, but some of the Louis XV furniture originally belonging to the MacVeaghs is still there. Of special note is the mantel made of eight different kinds of marble and holding Sèvres urns. The marine painting is by Clausell, a famous Mexican artist.

Two additional Clausell canvases and a watercolor scene of Washington, D.C., by General Antonio Betteta of Mexico City are in the spacious dining room, where most of the furniture dates to the MacVeagh residency.

The gayest area in the mansion is the solarium, which the Mexican government transformed completely in 1941 by covering the walls with famous Puebla tiles and adding a fountain. The colorful Talavera tiles feature the two great volcanoes of Mexico—Popocatepetl and Ixtacihuatl—and the coats of arms of the Republic and all the states of Mexico.

The residence has twenty-six rooms, two terraces, and nine baths. The palatial second floor can easily take care of more than a thousand reception guests, and frequently does, under the hospitable aegis of the current Ambassador, Hugo B. Margáin, and of Señora de Margáin.

A side of the solarium, with a fountain of Puebla tiles beneath a picture, produced in Talavera tiles, of Mexico's two great volcanoes.

120

The Turkish Embassy

Few embassies in Washington symbolize the magnificence and beauty of the nations they represent as strikingly as that of the Turkish Republic at 1606 Twenty-third Street, off Sheridan Circle.

This mansion, which houses both the Turkish chancery and the ambassador's residence, looks as if it were constructed to order by the country that bridges the West and the East, and has mingled the great cultures of both for centuries. With a splendor peculiarly its own, this great house is a masterpiece of design, craftmanship, and the arts, beautifully brought together from a variety of sources and a number of periods.

Yet it was not built to be a foreign property at all, but rather the home of an American multimillionaire in an era when palatial dwellings were status symbols and architects were encouraged to seek inspiration from abroad. George Oakley Totten, Jr., who, like John Russell Pope and Nathan C. Wyeth, designed several private mansions that became embassy residences, studied in Europe, and achieved signal success there before he planned this house.

One of his first noteworthy accomplishments abroad was in 1908 as architect for the first American chancery in what was then Constantinople (now Istanbul). He impressed the Turkish Prime Minister, Issaz Pasha, who asked Totten to design a house for him, and then invited him to stay on in Turkey to supervise a government construction project.

Totten declined. He had prior commitments in England and contracts pending in the United States. The Prime Minister came back with a second offer. Sultan Abdul-Hamid II wanted the talented young man to serve as his "personal and private" architect, at a tempting salary. Totten accepted, with the proviso that he be allowed to go first to England to discharge urgent business.

Three weeks later in London he learned that Abdul-Hamid had been deposed by the Young Turks, an organization of youthful liberals strongly opposed to his absolutism and intent on restoring the constitution, which he had long ignored.

The year was 1909. Totten, who had been away from the United States for three years, decided to return to Washington to pursue his career. His flair for designing great houses that looked as if they had been transported from the Old World synchronized with the tenor of the times in a pros-

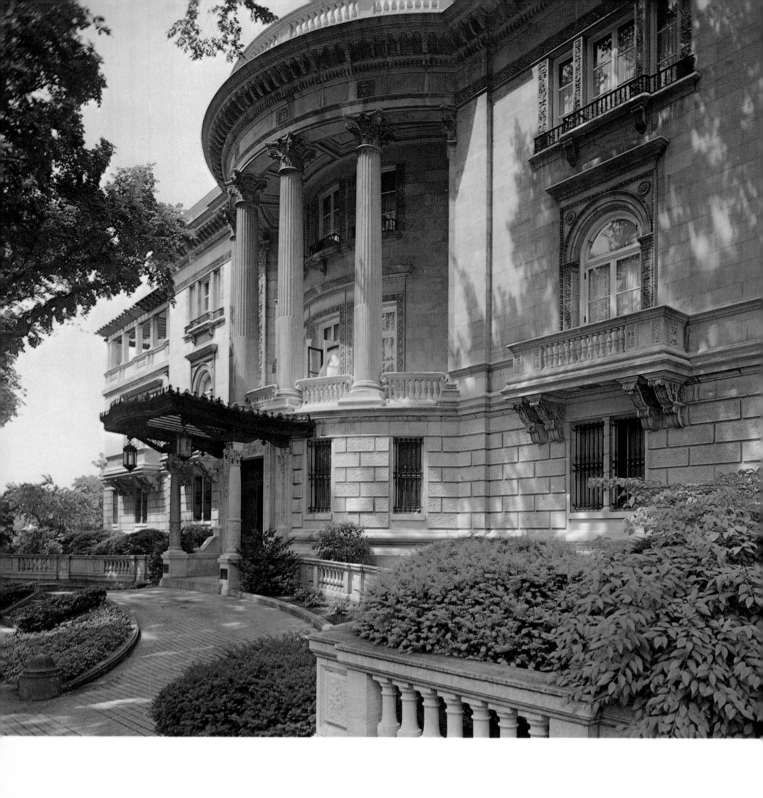

perous Capital city, and it was not surprising that Edward Hamlin Everett employed him to design a cost-no-object dwelling in 1914.

A multimillionaire philanthropist and industrialist, Everett had extensive Texas and Ohio oil holdings and was a large stockholder in a St. Louis brewing company; but he made the bulk of his fortune on a patent for the fluted top for soft drink bottles, and became widely known as "the bottle top king."

He already had homes in Vermont and Switzerland when he employed Totten to design the Washington house, and gave him free reign as to style and construction material. The result was a monumental, four-story stone structure of brick and Bowling Green granite, in the modified Roman Renaissance tradition.

Distinguished outside and in, the house facing Twenty-third Street has a colonnaded entrance, a partially suspended wrought-iron and glass portico, and a shallow driveway. The width of the structure ranges from ninety-one feet at its base to thirty-one feet at attic level, and sixty-six feet bordering Sheridan Circle to thirty-nine feet on the opposite side. The basement encloses the garage and a large swimming pool.

Bringing Louis XVI furniture, rich oriental rugs, and masterpieces of painting and sculpture, Everett and his family moved into the house in 1915. His wife died two years later.

In 1919, at a musical tea arranged by Mrs. John B. Henderson, he met the featured mezzo-soprano Grace Burnap, whom he married in 1920. From then until his death, their mansion was the frequent scene of gala "Evenings with Music," honoring American and European opera stars.

After Everett died in 1929, his widow lived there for a while, and then moved to Vermont. In 1932, the Turkish government leased the house with the option to buy. Meanwhile, the Turkish envoy and his staff continued to consider other available properties.

In 1933, when the choice was narrowed to the Everett house and a Sixteenth Street mansion, Ambassador Mehmet Munir Ertegun tipped the scales in favor of the former by writing to his government: "While many embassies are now located on Sixteenth Street, it is said that this area is more and more losing its value. Massachusetts Avenue is gaining more prominence."

The decision against Sixteenth Street must have disturbed the late Mrs. John B. Henderson, wife of a onetime senator from Missouri, even in her grave. From 1908 to 1929, she had waged a one-woman campaign to keep Embassy Row intact on the street she wanted to make Washington's most residentially distinguished thoroughfare. Largely because of her persistent pleas and political influence, she managed to get it designated "Avenue of the Presidents" by an Act of Congress on March 4, 1913; but the inappropriate appellation evoked such voluble criticism that Congress restored the name Sixteenth Street by an Act on July 21, 1914.

Doughty Mrs. Henderson was annoyed but not discouraged. She continued buying property in the vicinity of her fortress-like home, known as

Entrance of the
Turkish Embassy.

123

Henderson Castle, on Sixteenth Street at Florida Avenue, and promoting development where it would count as she wished. And like many other lobbyists before and since, she made the most of both her political and social contacts to accomplish her goal. One of her failures had to do with Everett, whom she entertained often while she was trying to sell him a site on Sixteenth Street in 1912. It was then that she introduced him to Totten, who had already designed big houses for her and was to do several more before she died.

Everett chose the Massachusetts Avenue area over Sixteenth Street; and so did the Turkish government, when in 1936 it bought the house and most of its valuable furnishings. Since then, a succession of envoys and their wives have added their own possessions to the interior from time to time, but there have been few basic changes in the house through the years. Today, therefore, it looks very much as it did when it was one of the city's most celebrated private dwellings.

A big iron-grille main doorway opens into a small vestibule, and another iron door leads to the big marble entrance hall, with its paneled walls, wide arches, Roman Doric pillars and pilasters, and a mantelpiece of carved white Italian marble holding two Capo di Monte urns. The white marble floor, bordered with colored mosaics, is partially covered by a rich oriental rug in shades of old rose and sienna.

To the left of the entrance hall are offices of the chancery. To the right is the ambassador's study, which Everett used as a poolroom. It is an attractive retreat today, with five oil paintings inset in the dark-paneled oak walls, two marble fireplaces, a Persian rug, and a big desk and tufted sofas and chairs, of which one set is upholstered in red velvet and the other in rose brocade.

Its ornate balustrade carved in a bell and fruit motif, the wide sweeping stairway leads to a landing, which was designed to be a music alcove and now is dominated by a huge bronze head of Mustafa Kemal Atatürk, founder of the Turkish Republic. Behind the sculpture is a stained-glass window in dramatic shades of green and blue, picked up by the mosaic-effect ceiling, which is frescoed with fanciful figures and inlaid with rare woods.

From the landing, a double staircase ascends to the enormous paneled reception room. Here the floor is of teakwood imported from China, and the ceiling, as in other rooms on this level, is elaborately decorated. The rug is Persian in rich shades of red, blue, and green. A massive, heavily carved mahogany table centers the room, which also has double chandeliers of crystal and ormolu. Typically Turkish is the enormous brass brazier near the windowed recess. The white marble fireplace with an elaborate chimney breast is flanked by doors opening into the drawing room.

Louis XVI furniture and a lovely little alcove help to make this one of the handsomest salons in Washington. The classic moldings, pilasters, and the pillars of the white walls complement white carved Italian mantelpieces, a pair of superb crystal chandeliers, gold damask draperies, an Aubusson rug in beige and old rose, two big Sèvres urns, and Louis XVI sofas, chairs, and

Bronze head of Atatürk dominating what was once a music alcove on the stairway landing.

The drawing room.

Opposite, top

The spacious second-floor reception hall.

Opposite, bottom

The dining room, shown with the table set for a small party, frequently accommodates as many as sixty guests for a seated dinner.

tables. Also here are some personal possessions of the current Ambassador and Mme. Esenbel, including a tenth-century Japanese screen, a Turkish scatter rug, and paintings of Istanbul by contemporary artists.

On the opposite side of the house, a double door from the reception room leads to the dining room, where heavily carved doorways and arches are relieved with white paneled walls. A charming decorative note on one is an ancient Korean figure painted on an oyster-white silk scroll in shades of green, the deepest tone blending with a nearby damask screen. Over the sideboard is a contemporary Turkish artist's portrayal of a scene in Central Anatolia.

Just off the dining room is a picturesque solarium, adorned with Turkish rugs, Byzantine tiles, stained-glass windows, and an intricate wrought-iron gate that opens into the ballroom. It is as luxurious as the throne room of a sultan's palace, with red velvet draperies, a satin-sheened hardwood floor, and mahogany wainscoting, surmounted by crimson and gold brocade panels that reach to the elaborate coffered ceiling.

A small sitting room containing Regency sofas and chairs upholstered in taupe velvet as well as a marble fireplace is on the same floor; the third floor has six large bedrooms—one with an adjoining sitting room—and four baths, and, over the ballroom, a roof garden, tiled and latticed, with an excellent view of the city. Servants' quarters are on the fourth floor.

127

The swimming pool in the basement has not been of much use in recent years, grand as it is. Some time after Everett's death, it was boarded up and remained closed for years. Ambassador Haydar Görk by chance discovered it one hot June day in 1955 and had it opened and cleaned, the basement walls and ceiling repainted, and fluorescent lights installed. But the pool has no water in it today, and the area around it is used for storage.

In preparation for the April, 1967, visit of the Turkish President Cevdet Sunay, the main floors of the embassy were repainted throughout, and Ambassador and Mme. Esenbel, who arrived earlier that year, added to the decor some of their personal possessions, including contemporary Turkish paintings and also exquisite Japanese screens and porcelains that they acquired in Tokyo, where the ambassador was *en poste* before returning to Washington for his second tour of duty. Very much in evidence, and a distinctive decorative note at the embassy today, are Mme. Esenbel's exquisite flower arrangements. The holder of eight diplomas from the three leading schools in which Ikebana is taught in Japan, she is an expert in the art.

The ornate ceilings, handsome boiserie, and fine furnishings of this mansion have luxurious addenda in gold-plated doorknobs, hinges, and other hardware throughout. All the appurtenances of tasteful luxury, in fact, abound in this embassy, which is Turkey in Washington today.

The ornate ballroom, with paneled and brocaded walls and a coffered ceiling.

128

The Irish Ambassador's Residence

Another onetime private Washington home that looks as if it had been built by the government that now owns it is the house of the Irish Ambassador at 2244 S Street. In fact, if it had been blueprinted in Dublin, this residence could not be more typical of the distinguished homes of Ireland.

It is comparatively small, but it is compact, with three floors and a basement including more than twenty rooms. In addition, it has a swimming pool, along with a broad terrace and a flourishing garden, from which a spectacular view of the city can be glimpsed over the treetops.

Designed by Waddy B. Wood, the house was constructed in 1924. The style may well have been chosen to fit in with that of several other dwellings in the vicinity, for John Russell Pope designed a whole row of Georgian dwellings for R and S streets from 1918 to 1922, and Wood was architect for the Georgian home built for Henry Parker Fairbanks at 2340 S Street in 1915 (later the last dwelling of the former President and Mrs. Woodrow Wilson).

The initial owner of what is now the Irish Ambassador's residence was Frederic A. Delano, an uncle of Franklin D. Roosevelt and a longtime Capital resident, who served on the Federal Reserve Board and then was chairman of the National Capital Park Planning Commission. In the 1930's, he and Mrs. Delano moved to an apartment on Sixteenth Street and sold the S Street property to Mrs. Reynolds Hitt, a member of a prominent Washington family, who lived there until her death at the age of ninety-two in 1965.

At the suggestion of Ambassador William P. Fay, the Irish government purchased the house in December of that year, and in August, 1966, he and Mrs. Fay moved into Ireland's first permanent residence in the nation's Capital. For some time, the Irish government had owned the chancery at 2234 Massachusetts Avenue, but a succession of envoys and their families had lived in leased Washington premises for more than forty years.

Finding a suitable house to buy was the prime order of business for Ambassador and Mrs. Fay when they arrived in Washington in the spring of

1964, shortly before the state visit of President Eamon de Valera. The temporary Irish Embassy residence then was the home owned by the George R. Renchards at 1743 Twenty-second Street. It had been the interim Presidential guest house during the 1963 renovation of Blair House. The Fays particularly liked the accessibility and convenience of the location.

After searching for months, they finally settled on the S Street house, just a few blocks away, because, in Mrs. Fay's words, "It was eminently suitable, being Irish Georgian—in the area we liked, and with grounds that would accommodate a swimming pool."

No sooner was the purchase completed than Mrs. Fay launched a thorough renovation program, employing Walter Mayo Macomber as architect. Not one to move hesitantly on any project, she was especially well prepared for this one. Her talent at house-finding, refurbishing, and furnishing had been shown during several of her husband's previous tours of diplomatic duty. She decorated an official Irish residence in Brussels, a sizable apartment in Stockholm, and a Paris house larger than the one in Washington.

She had the S Street residence lightened and brightened into a setting suitable for furnishings she and the ambassador owned, and others that would be needed. From their home in Dublin came a set of Louis XVI chairs and sofas, mirrors, and marquetry tables. Already in Washington were their grand piano (Mrs. Fay is a pianist of concert status), their eighteenth-century Irish silver and glass collections, and the ambassador's cherished assemblage of rare books.

While renovation on the house proceeded, Mrs. Fay began a protracted search for additional effects. For eight months she scoured antique shops in Washington and Ireland, and then augmented her purchases with pieces from government-owned Dublin Castle.

Ireland's Georgian mansion.

The task of transforming the house into a charming "bit of Ireland" with a few accents from other countries took a year and a half. Today, it is a truly elegant, moderate-sized mansion, in which each of the main rooms has a definite personality, and yet is a harmonious contributor to the distinctive whole.

Opening into the transverse main hallway, the vestibule has a marble floor, a Louis XV French commode surmounted by a *trumeau* mirror (with a painting in the upper section) and a Waterford crystal chandelier. Standing beneath the chandelier, one can glimpse the main salon and the terrace and garden beyond.

To the left of the vestibule is one of the most charming rooms in the house, the library, alive with vivid color keyed to the crimson carpet, beautifully bound French editions filling one wall, and a white marble Adam mantelpiece holding a pair of antique Chinese urns. The sconces here are of Waterford crystal. A satinwood Sheraton desk, a round marquetry table, easy chairs and a sofa, and a combination television receiver and high-fidelity phonograph are among other pieces in this cozy room, which obviously was designed for informal entertainment and small conversational groups.

Of special interest in the vestibule is the Louis XV commode, surmounted by a *trumeau* mirror.

The Irish emphasis is more noticeable in the appointments and rich delicacy of the drawing room. The dove-gray ceiling matches the walls, and the dado is of a slightly deeper shade. Three floor-to-ceiling windows on the terrace side give the salon a feeling of light and spaciousness. Shelved niches on either side of the fireplace show the glass collection. The classic mantelpiece, finished on either side with fluted pilasters and flanked by similar pilasters reaching to the cornice, has above it a portrait of Dolly Munroe, famed eighteenth-century Irish beauty, by Angelica Kauffmann.

Beautifully draped with deep valances, the aqua curtains are of Irish poplin. The Donegal carpet, woven to order for Mrs. Fay, is a stunning creation in shades of aqua, buff, and gray, designed with a double border and a motif of musical instruments near the center. Also in this attractive room are Louis XVI sofas and chairs, occasional tables, the grand piano, several pictures from the National Gallery of Ireland, and two mirrors framed in gilt filigree.

Curtains in the dining room are of the same material as those in the drawing room. The Donegal carpet, also designed to order, is patterned after an Aubusson rug in the Royal Palace of Laeken in Belgium. Walls of a soft terra-cotta shade have an off-white dado and trim, and the mantelpiece of black marble contrasts nicely with its brass fireguard and embers basket. Over the mantel is a study of a woman's head circled with a garland, by the seventeenth-century Italian painter Mario Nuzzi. The two other paintings in the room are by the noted Irish artist Nathaniel Hone, whose granddaughter, Evie Hone, created a stained glass window for the National Cathedral.

The graceful Waterford chandelier in the dining room centers over a mahogany three-pedestal table which, like the ladder-back chairs, was made by James Hicks of Dublin. The two eighteenth-century signed Sheraton sideboards are from Dublin Castle. Regency candlesticks, belonging to the Fays, are among the displayed pieces, which include an especially prized helmet-shaped sugar bowl made in 1800 by Peter Scott.

Four large bedrooms and four baths are on the second floor—the aqua suite and the gold suite are especially striking—and the third floor has eight bedrooms and two baths. A wine cellar, a game room equipped for table tennis, and storage rooms are in the basement.

This inviting Irish stronghold is one of the most popular locales in Washington. The dining-room table seats eighteen guests, and the main rooms open into each other. These, with the transverse hallways, can comfortably accommodate three hundred people. In warmer weather, with the terrace and gardens in use, as many as five hundred can be entertained at a time.

An inveterate gardener, Mrs. Fay is blessed with a green thumb. Her flower beds are works of art, carefully planned so that something will be blooming in season, with a profusion of lilies in the spring, summer, and autumn. They are just another of many delightful attractions of this official house, which has the charm of a private home.

The cozy library is a favorite before-and-after dinner locale.

133

The garden and
swimming pool from
the terrace.

Opposite, top

The drawing room.

Opposite, bottom

The dining room, an
ideal setting for Irish
hospitality at its best.

The Belgian Ambassador's Residence

While as serenely ordered as a European palace, the Belgian Ambassador's house at 2300 Foxhall Road is a splendid mélange incorporating French architecture and American limestone, antique furniture, art treasures from Europe and the Orient, and a superb view of the distant Virginia hills across the Potomac.

The main part of the mansion is a faithful reproduction of the eighteenth-century Hôtel de Charolais, 101 rue de Grenelle, Paris, which was built between 1700 and 1704 for the Marquis de Rothelin. It became known as the Hôtel de Charolais when it was occupied by Mademoiselle de Charolais, the Princess Louise-Anne de Bourbon-Condé.

With a frontage of 142 feet facing but set far back from Foxhall Road, the house has a depth of fifty-nine feet, thirty rooms on the first and second floors, and fourteen more for servants on the attic floor. Inspiration for the interior, with its richly paneled and carved walls, delicate crystal chandeliers, Aubusson carpets, parquet floors, and handsome furniture, was the eighteenth-century Château de Villarceaux, in France.

The mansion has been the property of the Belgian government since 1945, when Baron Robert Silvercruys was Ambassador to the United States. He and his beautiful American-born wife entertained often and distinctively, a practice that has continued to give the embassy special éclat under the current ambassador, Baron Louis M. Scheyven, and the Baroness Scheyven. The baroness has a flair for interior design, which is indicated by the success with which she handles flower arrangements, and the placement of furnishings to accentuate the key color in a room. The ambassador is a connoisseur, who on diplomatic tours of duty in China, Egypt, France, and Germany and on global trips has collected art objects that would enrich any setting.

The elegance of the interior is apparent from the moment one enters the front door. The main hall is floored with cream-colored Hauteville marble partially covered by an Aubusson carpet. The black and gilt *torchère* figures are reproductions of carvings by the famed French sculptor Clodion. Portraits by Isaac Luttichuys, which originally adorned either side of the entrance hall, were recently replaced by modern Chinese paneled paintings of plump chickens in one study and fishes in the other, from Ambassador Scheyven's private collection.

Faithfully duplicating one in the Château de Villarceaux, the main staircase in the house has a lacy balustrade and a graceful curve. Baroness Scheyven's fine feeling for color is shown in the big bouquet of blue phlox and delphinium that she has chosen to set off the Louis XV tables, and to blend with the powder-blue carpet that covers the floor in the stair hall. Two eighteenth-century Chinese ladies, painted on looking glass, flank the table, and a priceless collection of Chinese silk paintings decorates the wall on one side of the stairway.

A scarlet phoenix, emblem of the Chinese empress, is the painting that keynotes the color in the library. Designed after the George Hoentschel library, which the late J. Pierpont Morgan gave to the Metropolitan Museum, the room has Regency furnishings, along with priceless art effects, which, like the scarlet phoenix, are from the ambassador's own collection. Russian icons from the seventeenth and eighteenth centuries hang on either side of the mantelpiece, which is also framed by shelved niches displaying rare Chinese porcelain. Natural-finished oak, paneling the walls, is a mellow background for handsome bookbindings.

On the mantelpiece of mottled marble stands a Louis XV clock, and across the room an antique table supports a seventeenth-century wooden Madonna and Child from Liège, Belgium. A large, round marquetry table, with a center inlay of the Chinese symbol Fu (happiness) and five bats (for good luck) around the periphery, stands before the fireplace. Grouped around the table are overstuffed chairs and a sofa upholstered in rose and gold damask. A pair of Louis XVI period chairs with intricately carved backs and seats of red velvet, antique Chinese lamps, and an Italian Renaissance bronze figure are other exceptional pieces in the library.

Mme. Alphand, wife of a former French Ambassador to the United States, called the adjoining Louis XVI salon, "the most beautiful room in Washington." It is, indeed, a marvel of tasteful appointments in a spacious (forty-five-by twenty-five-foot) setting bound by soft gray-blue walls, paneled and carved. Beauvais tapestry covers the Regency chairs and sofas at one end of the room, and above the nearby mantelpiece are dainty Chinese statuettes of the Tang period (A.D. 618–907) —two dancers and six musicians. These remarkable little figures, which were buried for centuries in the coffin of a Chinese, were acquired by Baron Scheyven shortly after they were unearthed several years ago. The magnificent Aubusson rug and a blue petit point screen of the French Renaissance period are also of special interest in this room, as are *fauteuils*, upholstered in blue brocade to match a Regency sofa, and a Chinese Chippendale coffee table. Five ceiling-high French doors, including a double door in the center, open onto the terrace and offer a glorious glimpse of the Virginia hills across the Potomac River.

Eggshell-shaded walls with boiserie, into which a pair of eighteenth-century French landscape paintings have been set, are in the dining room. Niches display eighteenth-century terra-cotta figurines, and on a pedestal in one corner stands a sixteenth-century statue of St. George ready to spear a dragon.

The stairwell, with a bouquet of blue phlox and delphinium on the Louis XV table, and, on either side, a Chinese lady painted on glass.

The library, designed after a room in the Metropolitan Museum of Art, New York.

The graceful chandelier and the Aubusson carpet, similar to those in the other main rooms, enrich the setting for elegant—and sometimes sizable—dinners in the residence. Thirty persons can be seated at the Regency dining table. For larger dinners, five Chinese lacquer tables, which Ambassador Scheyven purchased years ago in Peking, are brought in to accommodate eight persons each. A second dining room, adjoining the main one, is also used when there are as many as a hundred dinner guests.

The house was built in 1931 for Raymond T. Baker on a property dubbed Baker's Acres, because it was comprised of thirteen (a baker's dozen) acres. Horace Trumbauer was the architect.

Once a Democratic candidate for the Senate, Baker was Woodrow

The Louis XVI salon, from the doorway to the dining room.

Opposite

In the salon, the mantel, surmounted by a handsome mirror and shelves displaying statuettes from the Tang period.

Wilson's Director of the Mint. His first wife, whom he married in 1918, was the Bromo-Seltzer heiress, Margaret Emerson, later the wife of Alfred Gwynne Vanderbilt. In 1928, Baker married Delphine Dodge, of the Detroit automobile family, shortly after she divorced James H. R. Cromwell.

Baker spared no expense in building and furnishing the Foxhall Road mansion. Indiana limestone seemed ideally suited for the exterior, paneling for the interior was imported from France, and the most modern facilities available were incorporated.

A setting for select dinners and soirees when the Bakers lived there, the house continued to draw distinguished guests later. After Baker died, it was occupied for a time by Dwight F. Davis, who had served as Secretary of War and Governor General of the Philippines, and Mrs. Davis. Mrs. Edward T. Stotesbury, mother of James H. R. Cromwell, leased it from her former daughter-in-law, Delphine Dodge Cromwell Baker Goode, in 1940.

Long acknowledged as the queen of Palm Beach society, Mrs. Stotesbury was equally active in Washington just before and during most of World War II. She entertained constantly, and her dinners and big receptions drew social, political, and diplomatic notables in droves. One of her biggest soirees almost coincided with tense wartime history. Scheduled as a "delayed birthday reception" for the then Senate Majority Leader Alben W. Barkley, it took place on December 7, 1941, a few hours after the jaw-shivering news of Pearl Harbor hit Washington. Foreign emissaries, high State Department officials, and enough members of the House and Senate to pass a congressional bill, were in the distressed throng that milled through the mansion's salons that evening, and wondered aloud whether there would be any more such big parties in Washington for quite awhile.

Mrs. Stotesbury saw to it that there were, however. Her social calendar continued at a lively pace through the war, and she stayed in the house—still known as the Baker House—until shortly before it was sold to the Belgian government in 1945.

As is often the case when a mansion goes into new ownership in Washington, the history of a house is reviewed by longtime interested residents. Several recalled that, while the Baker House was being built, an embarrassing incident in its connection involved a neighboring property of equal distinction—that of Mrs. J. Borden (Daisy) Harriman, later United States Minister to Norway, at 1800 Foxhall Road.

Mrs. Harriman had bought her house, then called Terrace Heights, and the three acres around it, in 1929. One of the oldest structures in the area, it was reputed to have been started long before the Revolution; but its official building date was recorded as 1774. It had become known as Spring Hill Farm when Henry Foxhall bought it in 1799. He added a substantial brick wing in 1880, and spent his summers there until he died in 1883. The property was owned by his descendants for a number of years, and during the Civil War, it became Battery Cameron, headquarters for the Maine artillery called in to defend the city of Washington. It also served briefly as a hospital; and it was during that period that a young lady from Maine, Lucy Wepley, arrived to visit a wounded relative. John Lightfoot, who lived on a

The dining room.

neighboring estate, met her and fell in love with her. After the war they married, and he bought Battery Cameron and reconverted it into a residence, where they lived for a number of years.

The place changed very little for more than a century; but an owner in the 1880's added a mansard roof, a two-tiered Victorian veranda, and a fancy cupola. Many other unattractive touches had been made in the structure when Mrs. Harriman bought the Victorian shell of a house, in which the interior had long since been stripped of all its valuable effects.

Working with a young Washington architect, James W. Adams, she launched an extensive renovation program. The entire lawn was built up, so that the view down the Potomac, as far as Hains Point, could be enjoyed. The mansard roof was replaced by a slate gable roof. The gingerbread verandas on the south were ripped off, and an arcaded portico entrance with wrought-iron railings was added. Old brick was used as much as possible for all additions, including the shallow brick wall which separated the upper lawn from the steep terrace below. Wide board from the old house went into the floor of the renovated version; all the windows were enlarged; paneling imported from England was put in the dining room; and the library was lined with American pine.

Mrs. Harriman named her house Uplands, and was completing the renovation in May, 1931, when workmen who were clearing the nearby Baker site dumped fifteen tons of dirt on her property. Mrs. Harriman and Raymond Baker were active fellow Democrats and good friends; however, on June 29, 1931, she sued him, his wife, and four others for fifteen thousand dollars on the grounds that the dirt, deposited without previous notice on her estate, had ruined the locale of a planned sunken garden. A settlement for a sum undisclosed to the public included removal of the dirt and the resumption of the Baker-Harriman friendship.

In the mid-1930's, Mrs. Harriman purchased a house in Georgetown, moved into it, and leased Uplands to a succession of distinguished residents. Speaker of the House and Mrs. William B. Bankhead and Senator and Mrs. John Bankhead took it in 1938. John Walker, director of the National Gallery of Art, and Mrs. Walker moved there in 1940. Mrs. Perle Mesta leased it for a year just before she became Minister to Luxembourg, but by that time it had a new owner, James Ryan, brother of Mrs. Parke Brady, who lived at 1801 Foxhall Road—and still does.

Ambassador W. Averell Harriman leased Uplands in 1952 and, later, Secretary of the Treasury and Mrs. George Humphrey were tenants for several years. It is now the residence of Dr. Emilio N. Oribe, the Uruguay Ambassador to the Organization of American States, and Señora de Oribe.

Incidentally, bricks for the original structure, which eventually became the house as it is today, were used as ballast for a ship that sailed from England the same year that John Foxhall came over to establish the Foxhall foundry in the countryside, a few miles from Georgetown. Eventually his name was to be given to the street, which was first known as Ridge Road, and which today passes by several outstanding Washington estates, in addition to the Belgian Embassy residence and Uplands.

The Peruvian Ambassador's Residence

Miles from the Foxhall Road area of fine houses is an embassy residence on a select site with historic connections. Located at 3001 Garrison Street, N.W., this architectural triumph, high on a wooded hill, is the dwelling of the Peruvian Ambassador. A cluster of chimneys and dormers, with ivy climbing over much of the exterior, gives the three-story Georgian structure a timeless appearance that blends into verdant, natural surroundings. The approach to the entrance winds through the twenty-five-acre property, which, more than a century ago, was Battery Terrill, a fortress set up for the defense of Washington during the Civil War.

The late Mr. and Mrs. Charles H. Tompkins built the house in the early 1920's. Favoring late Georgian architecture, they spent three years studying details of doorways, fenestration, and chimney placements in exemplary Delaware and Virginia residences before they completed plans. Mr. Tompkins liked the burnished taupe stonework of the old Pierce Mill in Rock Creek Park, and wanted his all-stone house to be of a similar shade and pattern. Mrs. Tompkins carefully selected the location of the house, so that it would not displace any of the natural battlements, the knolls, and hollows that had figured strategically at Battery Terrill. The firm of Incanti and Webel did the landscaping. Under architect Horace Peaslee, the house was completed in three years. There are teakwood floors of random-width boards and black walnut paneling in the library; an oval entrance hall, and spacious salons, library, and dining room on the first floor; bedroom suites and nine other rooms on the second, along with a large poolroom, which sometimes was used for dances.

At the suggestion of Peru's Ambassador Pedro Beltran in 1944, the Peruvian government bought the property. In succeeding years, the embassy residence was to become distinguished both as a social and diplomatic setting, and as a showcase for spectacular private collections.

Ambassador Fernando Berckemyer, who served on his first tour of duty in Washington from 1949 to the spring of 1964, and was Vice Dean of the Diplomatic Corps when he left, was fascinated with taurine art and owned the world's largest private assemblage of paintings, sculptures, lithographs, terra-cotta figurines, and books pertaining to the bullfight. More than a thousand items, accumulated over many years, were exhibited in his Washington embassy residence, while others filled a family museum in Lima. His

The driveway entrance of the Peruvian Ambassador's house.

Opposite, top
The drawing room.

Opposite, bottom
The sitting room, with paintings (now removed) from the private collection of the former Ambassador, Celsor Pastor.

extensive library had many valuable books on the subject, including his prized first edition of *De Toros y Toreros* (*Of Bulls and Bullfighters*), bound in red bull hide with onyx embellishments.

An entirely different kind of collection, in a refurbished setting, went on display in 1964, after Celsor Pastor arrived in Washington as Peruvian Ambassador. Before installing it, he and his wife, a sister of Peru's President Fernando Belaúnde Terry, had the residence suitably redecorated for their fabulous collection of Peruvian colonial art and centuries-old colonial furniture. Dark walls were painted a pale green, and wall-to-wall carpets in a

matching shade replaced the oriental rugs on the main floor. The library paneling was lightened, and furniture already in the drawing room was reupholstered in soft green, rose, and yellow fabrics.

The 1968 military *coup d'état* in Peru brought about the return of Fernando Berckemyer as Ambassador to the United States in December, and he and his wife, who had been making their home in San Francisco, moved back to the thirty-one-acre estate. Their own Spanish antique furnishings and fine paintings soon replaced those of their immediate predecessors; the residence was redecorated throughout; and the ambassador's assemblage of silver bulls again went on display, to the delight of his many friends in Washington.

During the tenure of the Pastors, Nan Robertson of *The New York Times* referred to the official Peruvian residence as the "jewel among embassies." At that period, it was a background for the finest private art collection of its kind in the world. It is equally distinguished today, as the dwelling of a *bon vivant* and his American-born wife, who are also notable collectors of art and antiques, as well as hosts with a gift of entertaining distinctively in the embassy which crowns one of the Capital city's most historic sites.

The dining room, with paintings (now removed) from former Ambassador Celsor Pastor's collection.

The hallway, showing the graceful main staircase.

148

IX

DURABLE DISTINCTION

1801 F Street, N.W.

To be "held in trust for the nation" by the National Trust for Historic Preservation, the Federal-style house at 1801 F Street, N.W., has been a Capital landmark since Chief Justice Marshall took up residence there in 1831.

Later, it was successively the home of a Maryland governor's daughter, Chief Justice Fuller, a countess, a prominent Washington attorney, an Illinois senator, and finally a distinguished New York representative whose widow, Mrs. Robert Low Bacon, has entertained the socially and politically elite there for more than forty years, and continues to do so. She has bequeathed the property to the National Trust to be administered as a museum after her death.

The exterior of the house is a charming period piece that challenges time. Of red brick with white lintels, dark-green shutters, and wrought-iron balconies, the four-story structure also has at the entrance a two-story bay, a sedate doorway, and two windows on the first floor proportioned similarly to the three windows immediately above.

Many styles mix and blend in the transitional atmosphere of the interior, which emphasizes comfort and convenience as well as beauty. Rooms with generous proportions and French and English period furnishings, intermingled with Chinese effects and sundry objects of art from many countries, give the house a cosmopolitan atmosphere in its traditionally American setting.

The magnificent, seven-foot mirror over a black marble mantel in the double drawing room recalls the past of the house, for worked into the elaborate gilt frame are carved animals—among them, an owl, a bear, and a crane—which Mrs. Bacon regards as symbols of some of the celebrated persons who have lived in the house. An elaborate work of art on several accounts, the mirror was created by Thomas Johnson, a contemporary of Thomas Chippendale II, who rivaled him in producing fanciful girandoles, sconces, and frames in the Gothic, Queen Anne, Chinese, and Louis XV

The entrance to Mrs. Robert Low Bacon's house, facing F Street

151

traditions. This piece, which has five candlesticks near the top, is a spectacular focus of interest in a house that has its share of treasures—and memories.

As is the case with a number of historic Washington dwellings, details of the origin of this house are obscure. Reliable sources indicate, however, that the lot originally belonged to Tobias Lear, President Washington's confidential secretary for sixteen years, who as early as 1791 asked Pierre Charles L'Enfant to purchase some land for him in what was to be the Capital city. Within six months, Lear acquired two lots. He built a home for himself on one—on the north side of H Street, between Eighteenth and Nineteenth streets—and sold the other at what is now F at Eighteenth, in 1797. Records do not indicate the buyer or the builder, but it has been established that the structure was begun in 1801, and that the owner when it was finished was Tench Ringgold. (Oddly enough, the street number today is 1801.)

Although described by a contemporary as "a fat and prosaic gentleman," Ringgold was active in the civic and political life of the new national Capital, which then numbered less than four thousand inhabitants. He managed a rope factory with some success, and was treasurer of the Georgetown Savings Institution. He also served as United States marshal of the District of Columbia, and in 1815, he was appointed to the commission in charge of rebuilding public edifices.

In the early decades of the Federal city, great private homes were few; boarding houses were numerous. With sessions of both Congress and the Supreme Court lasting only a few months of the year, many men of importance came to Washington without their wives, and took temporary lodging in houses not too far from Capitol Hill. Ringgold's daughter, who had inherited the F Street dwelling, ran it for paying guests; and among those who boarded there in the winter of 1831—and during the two succeeding winters—were Chief Justice Marshall and Associate Justice Joseph Story of Massachusetts. Marshall suggested to other colleagues on the Supreme Court that they also might like to stay there, but in one of his letters he wrote that the location of the house "between the palace and Georgetown" might be too far from the court to suit some members. (His reference to "the palace," meaning the White House, was an obvious gibe at President Jackson with whom Marshall was constantly at odds.)

Justice Story wrote that he and Marshall kept "bachelor hall at the house in the most frank and unaffected intimacy," and added, "Our social hours, when undisturbed with labors of the law, are passed in gay and frank conversation."

At least once a week, some of the other justices shared relaxed conversation with them, for Marshall frequently had as Sunday-dinner guests Associate Justices Henry Baldwin of Connecticut, Smith Thompson of New York, and John McLean of New Jersey. Marshall's fellow Virginian Senator Henry Clay also was often present.

Prominent in the national picture even before President John Adams appointed him to head the Supreme Court in 1800, Chief Justice Marshall was one of the most revered officials in Washington in those days. At a Sunday dinner at the F Street house in 1832, he was reputed to have men-

Chinese ancestral portraits, surveying the stair hall on the main floor.

Part of the double
drawing room showing
the elaborate mirror
over the mantel
(*right*).

The portrait of four-
year-old Virginia
Murray (Mrs. Bacon),
the Chinese screens, and
an oriental obelisk on
the table are items of
special interest in the
dining room.

tioned to five of his colleagues that he had been a national public servant for thirty-five years—against his will. He went on to recall that in 1795 he turned down President Washington's offer to make him Attorney General and the appointment to succeed James Monroe as Minister to France the following year, on the grounds that he wanted to continue the private practice of law and felt that calling "to be more independent but not less honourable than any other." (However, in 1797, President John Adams urged him to go to Paris as one of three commissioners to adjust differences between the young republic and the government of France, and he accepted. Then he served as Secretary of State for less than a year before his appointment as Chief Justice.)

Marshall and Story were boarders at the F Street establishment for only three winters, but the luster they brought to it continued to glow for years. In 1836, Governor Sprigg of Maryland bought the property for his daughter, Mrs. William Thomas Carroll, and her husband, a clerk at the Supreme Court.

Known as the Carroll House for almost sixty years, the dwelling was a gathering place for prominent Marylanders and Washington officialdom. It became even more socially prestigious after Chief Justice Melville Fuller purchased it in 1896.

President Cleveland's appointee to succeed Chief Justice Morrison R. Waite, Fuller had headed the Supreme Court for six years when he decided to move his family from Maine to Washington. His inventory indicated that he and his wife had amassed quantities of furnishings; more than enough to fill the four floors of their newly acquired house. So they had a small addition constructed on the west side and the two-story bay on the south; and they glassed in the long porch on the back. (One of the most inviting rooms in the house today, this sunny retreat is a museum within itself, full of exceptional furnishings and priceless bibelots.)

Chief Justice and Mrs. Fuller were gregarious but selective. Their receptions and dinners flourished around the highest echelons of their time. Even though less distinguished than Marshall, Fuller was a genial and brilliant man. He and his wife moved with ease and frequency in both official and social circles, and his eminence was emphasized in 1899, when President McKinley appointed him as a member of the arbitration commission sent to Paris to settle the Venezuela-British Guiana boundary dispute.

After Fuller's death in 1910, his family returned to Maine; and the Countess of Yarmouth (later, Mrs. Geoffrey Whitney) bought the house. The former Alice Cornelia Thaw, a sister of Harry K. Thaw, she had married the Earl of Yarmouth in Pittsburgh in April, 1903, and divorced him five years later, but she was still using the title when she bought the Washington property in 1910.

During the next two years, she executed a complete renovation program. The walls were plastered and lightened, magnificent gas chandeliers and black marble mantels were installed, and a powder room and coatroom were constructed on the entrance floor. But her rich furnishings were hardly in place when she decided to lease the property, with most of its effects.

Socially prominent Mrs. Harold Walker, wife of an internationally known attorney, presided over the house in 1912. Illinois Senator and Mrs. Medill McCormick were living there during the time the League of Nations controversy was the Number One topic in Washington, and arguments about it enlivened many of their important dinner parties. Representative and Mrs. Bacon, who arrived in Washington with the Coolidge administration, leased the house for two years, and had already made it a gathering place for social and political notables before they purchased it in 1925.

Possessing quite an assemblage of English and American furniture, paintings, and art objects of their own, the Bacons needed comparatively few of the effects already there, but among those they did buy were the spectacular mirror, the exquisite brass chandeliers, and the bright red rugs in the double drawing room. However, Mrs. Bacon failed to acquire one piece she very much wanted, a graceful clock, gay with chinoiserie motifs, that stood in the second-floor hallway. The former Countess of Yarmouth declined to sell it; but a handsome substitute was forthcoming—a clock imaginatively decorated with Chinese designs and, coincidentally, bearing on its face in big black letters, *Yarmouth*. A gift from Mrs. Bacon's mother, it had been purchased some years before in England.

Every room on the main floor is full of antique treasures. Mrs. Bacon has a special fondness for the oriental. She once won the Peking Sweepstakes, and spent most of the small fortune on Chinese items; and she has been collecting them ever since. Her house today has enormous Chinese ancestral portraits on the walls of the stair hall. Eight Chinese immortals in porcelain adorn one of the drawing-room mantelshelves. Distributed through the main rooms and in the small sitting room to the left of the stair hall are the components of numerous noteworthy collections from many countries— Chinese screens, Tang figurines, jade, miniature portraits, bronzes, rare china and silver, carved ivories, and chess sets in a wide variety of rare woods and unique designs.

Teakwood tables, sturdy English, French, and American sofas and chairs, upholstered in opulent fabrics, and Chinese Chippendale pieces blend gracefully in a setting that is at once an invitation to the past, and a reminder that truly beautiful possessions defy time and may be even more highly cherished in the future.

Among many items that attract special attention is a side chair that belonged to one of Mrs. Bacon's ancestors, John Murray, Earl of Dunmore, who was the last royal governor of Maryland. Along with his portrait, those of other ancestors and contemporary relatives abound on walls of the main rooms. An engaging portrait of Virginia Murray (Mrs. Bacon at the age of four) hangs over the mantelpiece in the dining room. In the adjoining sunroom, two sculptures are notable—one is Malvina Hoffman's study of Robert Low Bacon; the other is of his father, Robert Bacon, onetime Secretary of State and then Ambassador to France, by James Earle Fraser.

The kitchen and pantry of the house are on the ground floor. In addition to the seven rooms on the main floor, there are twelve rooms—a library, Mrs. Bacon's suite, and guest rooms—on the third floor, and ten rooms on the

fourth. Upper and lower galleries on the west side of the house have ornamental wrought-iron railings and a staircase that Mrs. Bacon installed to lead to the walled garden.

The house has served its purpose admirably. Carrying out the tradition set by Chief Justice Marshall, it was a political and social center up until the time of Mr. Bacon's death in 1938; and so it has continued to be. For years, the house was the scene of suppers after the annual Gridiron dinners, when political talk ran high; of dinners enlivened by stimulating discussion when the division of Palestine was the prime topic of debate; of dinners before and suppers after official conferences when the United Nations was being formulated. Virtually every controversy involving America and the world has reverberated through this house since the Bacons moved into it.

With the property, which also includes a stable and a coach house, Mrs. Bacon has bequeathed to the National Trust "the furniture necessary to preserve the character of the main floor of the house." She hopes the museum to be established will be "a living museum," a center for forum discussions of important topics of the day. She would like them to be directed by a council headed by the Chief Justice, and including cultural, political, and civic leaders. In other words, she hopefully visualizes her home as continuing the tradition of intellectual hospitality that it has enjoyed in the past. "It is a house," she has said, "that wants to be amused."

The house as seen from the walled garden on the west.

159

Decatur House

The Decatur House, at 748 Jackson Place, and the Woodrow Wilson House, at 2340 S Street, are properties of the National Trust. The former had a distinguished history revolving around many important persons.

It was built by Commodore Stephen Decatur, who was noted for his service in the War of 1812 and in suppressing the Barbary Pirates in the Mediterranean. He arrived in Washington in 1815 on appointment to the Naval Board of Commissioners, and shortly afterward bought land at the northwest corner of Lafayette Square (then known as the President's Square).

Wanting a home in which he could entertain his socially and politically elite friends, Decatur employed the best architect he could find—Benjamin Latrobe, who produced plans for a structure with the restrained elegance of the Regency or Federal periods.

Stephen and Susan Wheeler Decatur were delighted. The house was finished in 1818, and early in 1819 they moved in with their valuable furnishings, paintings, and memorabilia of the commodore's achievements.

As great houses went in those days, their new dwelling was not large, with only fifty-one feet on Lafayette Square and forty-five feet on H Street, but it had a full basement, three stories, and an attic, as well as servants' quarters and a carriage house at the rear.

Attractive and hospitable, the Decaturs entertained often and distinctively, and were highly popular in Washington's most exclusive circles.

The final party given by the Decaturs was a dinner honoring President and Mrs. Monroe's daughter Maria and Samuel Lawrence Gouverneur who had been married at the White House nine days before. The event at Decatur House was the gayest and most lavish social affair of the season, but several guests were to recall later that the host was preoccupied, even morose, through most of the evening. He had reason to be. He had been challenged to a duel, and the date had been set.

His adversary was Commodore James Barron, an erstwhile fellow naval officer, who was suspended from service after surrendering his ship, the

Decatur House, on
Lafayette Square.

161

Chesapeake, to British frigate *Leopold* before the War of 1812. The captain of the *Leopold* demanded surrender on the charge that Barron's ship carried three crewmen who were British deserters. Barron complied without firing a shot. As a result, he was suspended from naval service and put on half pay for five years. When he sought reinstatement, Decatur, who had sat on Barron's court martial, opposed his plea. Barron's challenge to a duel, which grew out of correspondence relative to the plea, was delivered to Decatur on March 8, his fourteenth wedding anniversary, through Captain Jesse Elliott, Barron's second. Commodore William Bainbridge served as Decatur's second when the duel took place on the early morning of March 22, 1820, at the Bladensburg, Maryland, dueling grounds. Decatur, mortally wounded, died a few hours after—in Decatur House.

His widow, moving shortly afterward to Kalorama, the Bromford residence near Florida Avenue and Sixteenth Street, stayed there for some time and then took up residence in Georgetown at 2812 N Street, the former home of Judge James Morsell, where she spent the remainder of her life.

For the next few years, the house on Lafayette Square was rented to a succession of prominent tenants, beginning with the French Minister Jean Guillaume, Baron Hyde de Neuville, whom a colleague described as "a most estimable man with a kind wife who enjoys making others happy." The Russian Minister Baron de Tuyll, the next tenant, suffered from gout and preferred seclusion, but his infrequent dinners were noted for their excellent fare, and he was to be remembered by his summation of Capital cuisine: "Washington with its venison, wild turkeys, canvasbacks, oysters, terrapins, etc. furnishes better viands than Paris, and only wants cooks."

Following the Russian Minister, Secretary of State Henry Clay moved to Decatur House, and furnished it handsomely with French pieces. The next occupant was Clay's successor as Secretary of State, Martin Van Buren, under whose aegis the house became a political nerve center for the campaign to win social acceptance for controversial Peggy O'Neale Eaton.

Edward Livingston, the succeeding Secretary of State, was another tenant of Decatur House. He and his wife made glittering social history, and crowned their careers as hosts with a brilliant wedding ceremony for their daughter Cora, who was hailed as the "queen of American society," after she married Thomas P. Barton of Philadelphia in 1833.

Sir Charles Vaughan, the British Minister, and Lady Vaughan were occupants from 1834 through most of 1835. The following year, the house was purchased by John Gadsby, a builder and hotelkeeper who was suspected of slave trading (indeed, one widely circulated rumor was that he was conducting slave auctions on the premises). But, in any event, Gadsby furnished the house lavishly, and continued to live there in splendor until his death in 1844.

Vice President George Mifflin Dallas leased Decatur House from Gadsby's widow, refurbished it from cellar to attic, and reestablished its social preeminence. After Dallas returned to Philadelphia, the dwelling underwent many changes. For two years it was an apartment house, attracting several members of Congress. Representative William Appleton of

The original sitting room of the mansion, opening into the dining room.

The bedroom in Decatur House, in which Commodore Stephen Decatur died.

Massachusetts then leased it for a time, and later, Secretary of the Treasury Howell Cobb. Louisiana's Senator Judah P. Benjamin, the next tenant, filled the house with elaborate furnishings in an effort to lure his wife back from France. Returning briefly, she was chilled by her reception in Washington and fled again to Paris, taking their eighteen-year-old daughter with her. Not long after leaving the Capital, Benjamin wrote that he had known "the deepest sorrow in the house that I prepared for my greatest happiness."

During the Civil War, the Federal government took over Decatur House, along with others in the area. Afterward, General Edward F. Beale purchased it, repaired it extensively, and made some additions.

In 1876, President Grant appointed Beale as envoy to Austria-Hungary. With his son Truxtun as his personal secretary, he remained abroad a year, and returned to Washington hoping that President Arthur would appoint him Secretary of the Navy. From then until his death, he and Mrs. Beale were socially active, and invitations to their dinners, receptions, and musicals were eagerly sought. The general died in 1893 and, in 1902, upon the death of Mrs. Beale, their son Truxtun inherited Decatur House.

Living in California at the time after having served as Minister to Persia and then Greece, he did not move to Washington at once. Indeed, it was not until 1912 that he returned East with his second wife (his first was Harriet Blaine, the daughter of James G. Blaine from whom he was divorced in 1896) to reside in Decatur House.

For the next forty-four years, Decatur House was to be one of the most important locales in Washington society. Mrs. Beale, the former Marie Chase Oge of California, had the mansion restored in the 1930's under the direction of Thomas Tileston Waterman. The Victorian accents that had been added inside and out by General Beale were removed in a successful effort to recapture the mood and details of Latrobe's original architecture. Major alterations in the interior included replacement of the Victorian dining furniture with English pieces, circa 1800, such as would have suited the house just after it was built; the addition of other items of the period, such as a copy of one of President Washington's desks; and the changing of the Victorian library into a room for displays relating to the history of the house.

Truxtun Beale died in 1936. His widow continued to maintain her status as an outstanding hostess, who sometimes gave dinners at the suggestion of the State Department, and each year presided over a full calendar of select social functions, including a supper party after the annual White House reception in honor of the Diplomatic Corps.

Marie Beale died in 1956, two years after publication of her book, *Decatur House and Its Inhabitants*. A more recent book, *Decatur House*, published by the National Trust, tells an even more complete story of this landmark, its background, furnishings, the personalities who inhabited it through the years, and its use today as both a museum and headquarters of the National Trust.

The Woodrow Wilson House

The Woodrow Wilson House, where both the twenty-eighth President of the United States and his widow died, was built for Henry Parker Fairbanks in 1915. A red brick Georgian structure, it was designed by Waddy B. Wood. Mrs. Wilson, who selected it as a suitable residence near the end of her husband's second White House term, later described it as "an unpretentious, comfortable, dignified house, fitted to the needs of a gentleman."

Shortly after purchasing it, the Wilsons installed an elevator, a billiard room, iron gates at the entrance to the drive, and a brick garage. Several partitions were changed in the interior, and shelves were built to take care of Wilson's extensive library.

Immediately after the inaugural ceremonies for President Harding on March 4, 1921, the Wilsons went to the house where they were to spend the remainder of their lives. In *My Memoirs*, Edith Bolling Wilson gives an account of their arrival:

> This house, which forty-eight hours before I had last seen in utter confusion, was in perfect order—curtains and pictures hung, rugs down, and flowers, flowers, flowers everywhere. Every room a bower and a sense of home and peace pervading rooms that otherwise would have seemed unfamiliar. The place looked as if we had been there for years.
>
> On the threshold of his room my husband leaned on his cane to survey another miracle. Every article was in the relative position it had occupied at the White House; all the little things . . . and the extraordinarily large bed that had been made to order, and which Mr. Wilson had especially desired . . .

Before her death in 1961, Mrs. Wilson had specified that the house was to be presented to the American people under guardianship of the National Trust; visitors to the museum today can see many of the possessions which the last inhabitants of the house held dear. There is a chair which was used by the President at Cabinet meetings, and which bears a bronze plaque presented by members of his Cabinet. By the library fireplace is an easy chair inscribed with a card in Wilson's handwriting: "Presented to my dear wife, whose inspiration meant so much to me while I occupied this chair. Woodrow Wilson."

Particularly inspiring is the content of the library, which features numerous books inscribed to Wilson, and rare and richly bound presentation volumes of the Wilsonian era. Also of special interest are the Gobelin tapestry ("The Marriage of Psyche," woven specifically for President and Mrs. Wilson), autographed portraits, paintings, commemorative china, and antiques owned by Mrs. Wilson's family.

The bedroom in which Woodrow Wilson died.

X

MODERN ACCENTS ON FOXHALL ROAD

The Cafritz House

When the late Morris Cafritz, Washington builder and philanthropist, built his rambling white brick contemporary residence at 2301 Foxhall Road in the 1930's, it was the most modern great house in the Capital city. On a seven-acre site, giving a breathtaking view of Georgetown and Washington, it was designed by the owner, who patterned it partially after a contemporary mansion created in Mt. Kisco by Edward Durell Stone. Eugene Schoen assisted in selecting the fine woodwork used throughout the house and also to accentuate the handsome entrance door.

The mansion has a long driveway winding in from Foxhall Road; and, on the opposite side, a large terrace, a formal garden, and a rolling lawn that extends well beyond the swimming pool. The interior is furnished in the contemporary style, and the long rectangular living room, adorned with modern imported tapestries, the spacious dining room, and the terrace are familiar to many partygoing Washingtonians.

The Kreeger House

Next door to the Cafritz estate is the most spectacular new complex in Washington, the ultramodern home of Mr. and Mrs. David Lloyd Kreeger, which also houses their extraordinary collection of paintings and sculpture.

Designed by Philip Johnson and Richard Foster, the dwelling is an architectural masterpiece. Tons of Italian travertine, the beige limestone that adorns many palaces, went into the walls, floors, and terraces that dominate five and a half wooded acres. Glass walls and vertical grilles accent the structure, designed with a series of twenty-two-foot modules conjoining a great hall (sixty-six feet long, twenty-five feet high), with a sitting room,

The Kreeger House,
designed by Philip
Johnson and Richard
Foster.

View of the Kreeger
House showing the
vertical grilles that
mark the great hall,
the domed roofs, and
the one-story entrance.

168

library, dining room and kitchen, master bedroom, two guest rooms, and servants' quarters.

The spacious house is an ideal setting for the Kreegers' treasures, which John Walker of the National Gallery of Art has hailed as "one of the truly distinctive collections of impressionist and post-impressionist art, put together with great taste."

The triple-domed central hall, which also serves for chamber-music concerts (both the Kreegers are accomplished musicians), was designed for the Cézannes and Renoirs in the collection. The one-story entrance hall is hung with paintings by Gauguin, Bonnard, and Degas. Eight Monets are in the double dining room. In the stair hall, a Miró and a Kandinsky flank the window that affords a view of the conservatory. Also displayed in the main rooms of the house are works of Van Gogh, Picasso, Moreau, Chagall, Braque, and Matisse. Three large rooms on the ground level are galleries featuring twentieth-century American art, African paintings, and a collection of African shells.

The sculpture collection—works of Moore, Maillol, Lipschitz, and Arp—are at home on the terrace, protected by a travertine and Plexiglass canopy. The terrace overlooks a sixty-six foot swimming pool.

A ten-foot concrete wall on Foxhall Road and a fence on the woodland side of the house provide protection and privacy for this museum-home, which has been described as "the finest house to be built in Washington in the twentieth century."

Opposite

The great hall. Seen through the window is the Maillol sculpture that dominates the outdoor court.

Entrance hallway, with paintings by Gauguin, Bonnard, and Degas.

XI

ONCE-PRIVATE HOUSES

The depression of the late 1920's, the steadily worsening servant problem, and the increasing but more transient population since World War II have prompted numerous builders and inheritors of Washington mansions to dispose of them. Several great houses have been demolished to make way for apartment and office buildings. A few have been sold to foreign governments. More have been purchased to serve as exclusive clubs, organization headquarters, or museums.

Dumbarton House

Bays at the rear of Dumbarton House overlook a garden designed by Fiske Kimball.

One of the earliest mansions in Georgetown is Dumbarton House, which was called Bellevue for more than a hundred years before the National Society of Colonial Dames of America acquired it from Colonel John Newbold in 1928. Dating to the eighteenth century, it now serves as headquarters for the National Society as a museum of colonial Americana.

Located at 1715 Q Street in Georgetown, it was restored in 1931 by Horace W. Peaslee with Fiske Kimball of the Pennsylvania Museum of Art as adviser. Kimball described it when completed as "one of the most beautiful houses of its kind in America." It does not stand on its original site; the name of the builder cannot be verified; and the house was known successively as Dumbarton, Bellevue, and Rittenhouse Place before it became Dumbarton House. Because of uncertainty as to its initial architecture and the alterations that have taken place since, the restored house has no claim to fidelity of period, but it is impressively characteristic of fine dwellings in the late Georgian or early Federal tradition.

Of red brick trimmed in white, the two-story structure has a pedimented central section with a white portico supported by Doric columns and a paneled entrance door with fretted sidelights and fanlight. The window directly above follows the same general pattern, its quoins defining the curved top; the crowning fanlight partially framed by a pediment is similarly

The central hallway.

The delicate Georgian
plaster cornices and
the carved wood
mantelpiece in the
main sitting room.

designed. Four tall windows with white lintels—and two on the second floor with delicate wrought-iron balconies—flank the center of the façade. A corbeled cornice and low service wings on either side of the house further accent the structure, which stands on a rise above the sidewalk level and is approached by a flight of stairs cut into the retaining wall.

The interior design is typical of colonial America. The wide central hall opens into four large rooms. The two at the front are square; the two to the rear have bay windows overlooking the terraced garden and its high brick wall. Fiske Kimball designed the garden, which has as the central motif a circular bench and a graceful niche. The flower beds are typical of those in Georgetown gardens in the early 1800's.

In the main rooms, delicate Georgian plaster cornices and carved wood mantelpieces are complemented with furniture made between 1780 and 1810, and approved by furniture historian Luke Vincent Lockwood. Peale and Stuart portraits accent walls of the dining room and parlor; and all the handsomely bound books in the library date before 1810. An exhibition room on the second floor features china, glass, bric-a-brac, and clothing that once belonged to George and Martha Washington, the latter's granddaughter Mrs. Thomas Law, Dolley Madison, George Mason of Gunston Hall, and Lord Fairfax of Greenway Court.

The first owner of the site was Ninian Beall, who came to this country as an indentured servant and won acclaim as an Indian fighter. As a reward, Queen Anne in 1702 granted him 795 acres on Rock Creek.

He named the tract "Rock of Dumbarton," after the Rock of Dumbarton in his native Scotland, and lived to see it through its initial stages of division. Subsequent owners of the site, several of whom were prominently identified with the history of Georgetown, were Ninian Beall's son George, Georgetown's Mayor Peter Casanave, General Uriah Forrest, Isaac Pollock, Samuel Jackson (who probably built the original house), Gabriel Duval (Comptroller of the Currency and later Supreme Court Justice, who bought the property for taxes in 1804), Joseph Nourse (Registrar of the Treasury, who remodeled the house according to Benjamin Latrobe's design), and Charles Carroll (who bought it in 1813).

Carroll named the house Bellevue and, copying his brother who was known as Daniel Carroll of Duddington, called himself Charles Carroll of Bellevue. A friend of James and Dolley Madison, Carroll escorted the latter on her flight from the burning White House in 1814. They stopped briefly at Bellevue, where she wrote a letter describing her rescue of Gilbert Stuart's portrait of George Washington, while waiting for the President to join her.

In 1816, members of the Rittenhouse family of Philadelphia purchased the house, and it was known as Rittenhouse Place until 1890. The next owner, Horace Hinckley, sold it to Colonel John L. Newbold in 1912. Three years afterward, when plans were under way to open up Q Street, the house, which long had blocked direct transit from Washington proper to Georgetown, was moved to its present location. The operation was difficult. Wings of the house had to be taken down and set up again brick by brick; but the central part with its original portico and cornice remained intact.

Pages 176–177

Every item in the stately dining room is of museum status.

The library features a bookcase with a collection of handsomely bound volumes, all dating before 1810.

Like all furnishings in the main part of the house, those in the bedrooms were made between 1780 and 1810.

Dumbarton Oaks

The Capital city's nearest approximation to the Palace of Versailles is Dumbarton Oaks, another landmark with a history linked to Ninian Beall, for its Georgetown site also was once part of the "Rock of Dumbarton." Today a research center of Harvard University, the property is dominated by a Georgian mansion, which encloses a vast research library and collection, paintings, sculptures, tapestries, and furnishings—all given to Harvard by Ambassador and Mrs. Robert Woods Bliss in 1940.

The main structure and the wing that was added in 1963 house a library of fourteen thousand volumes dealing primarily with Byzantine civilization. The collection constitutes the only museum in the United States devoted exclusively to early Christian and Byzantine art. The new wing, designed by Philip Johnson, is devoted primarily to the pre-Columbian art assemblage of the late Robert Woods Bliss, who served abroad in several diplomatic posts, and was Ambassador to Argentina just before he retired in the early 1930's.

The estate includes an orangery in the original greenhouse, a brook with a waterfall, an orchard, and a yew-lined walk, as well as a swimming pool and tennis courts screened by wisteria and rhododendron. Also extant are picturesque remnants of the self-contained estate it was more than a century ago—a waterwheel and a millstone, a caretaker's house, and stables. Truly spectacular today, the terraced gardens contain centuries-old boxwood, romantic fountains, a mosaic pool, and flowering shrubs and trees that cover six acres, and are monuments to the vision and taste of the late Mrs. Bliss.

The main entrance of Dumbarton Oaks.

The original house was built in 1801 by William Hammond Dorsey, who bought the land from Thomas Beall. So handsome that his intimates called him "Pretty Billy," Dorsey was also brilliant and versatile. He was serving as President Jefferson's first judge of the Orphans Court when he designed and directed the building of his mansion. Its central hall was said to be wide enough "for a wagon to pass through." He named the property The Oaks.

Pebble mosaics,
romantic fountains,
and flowering shrubs
distinguish the terrace
garden.

180

A number of owners and tenants occupied the house, and it changed names three times from 1805, when Dorsey sold it to Robert Beverly, until 1920 when the Blisses bought it. Beverly's son James called it Acrolophus (Greek for "grove on the hill"). Later owners included James E. Calhoun, who turned the property over to his distinguished brother Vice President John C. Calhoun in time for the latter to entertain Lafayette during his 1824 visit to the United States.

Brooke Mackall acquired the property in 1826. Edward Magruder Linthicum bought it twenty years later, and promptly renamed it Monterrey in memory of his son who was killed in the great battle of the Mexican War. Colonel Henry M. Blount, who became owner in 1891, restored its original name. Ambassador and Mrs. Bliss gave it the even more fitting title—Dumbarton Oaks.

The house had undergone many alterations and additions by the time the Blisses bought it. Linthicum, particularly, had made noticeable changes by installing a mansard roof and adorning the façade with classic pediments, cornices, and carved stone ornaments. Mr. and Mrs. Bliss completely transformed the grounds into a majestically landscaped setting and made many improvements in the house. In 1929, they added the music room; and it was there in the late summer of 1944 that the historic Dumbarton Oaks Conference, a forerunner of the United Nations organization, took place.

An exhaustive story of the past and present of the mansion and grounds is given in *Dumbarton Oaks, the History of a Georgetown House and Garden, 1800–1966,* by Walter Muir Whitehill, librarian of the Boston Athenaeum. Even enthusiasts who are familiar with the estate will view it with renewed appreciation after reading his comprehensive account.

The music room, scene of the Dumbarton Oaks Conference in 1944.

Belmont House

Among the earliest mansions in Washington proper is the one now called Belmont House, headquarters of the National Woman's Party at 144 B Street, N.E. Its Capitol Hill site was part of the original grant of land to Lord Baltimore in the 1600's, and the property today incorporates a house believed to have been built as early as 1750.

The land was inherited by Daniel Carroll of Duddington, who presented his thousand-acre farm to the Federal city in 1799. Robert Sewall, scion of an illustrious Maryland family, bought from Carroll and the city the lot on which the present house stands. Already on the site was a house believed to have been built in 1772 by the third Lord Baltimore as a wedding gift for his daughter.

Using the existing structure as a kitchen wing, Sewall built the sizable home which was to play a dramatic role in history. It was finished in 1800, but shortly afterward Sewall inherited Poplar Hill, a vast Maryland estate, and moved there, leasing his Capitol Hill house to Albert Gallatin, Secretary of the Treasury.

A background for gracious living for almost fourteen years, the home was also a gathering place for government leaders. Henry Adams in his *Life of Albert Gallatin* implied that the convenient location of the dwelling brought its occupant into close relationship with members of Congress, and added:

> The principal adherents of the Administration were always on terms of intimacy in Mr. Gallatin's house, and much of the confidential communication between Mr. Jefferson and his party in the Legislature passed through this channel.

Secretary Gallatin and his family lived there until 1813, when President Madison appointed him Commissioner to Russia. The Sewalls again took possession of the house, but they were at Poplar Hill on August 24, 1814, when British forces under General Ross and Admiral Cockburn advanced on Washington and were greeted with a fusillade from the Sewall mansion. Enraged when his horse was killed, General Ross ordered that the house be burned. The damage, while difficult to assess now, may have been extensive, but Sewall promptly had the structure rebuilt to its former design.

Façade of Belmont House.

185

Busts and portraits of famed feminists line the walls of the central hallway.

The sitting room, with treasured Victorian effects.

He died in 1820, leaving the property to his widow. In time, it descended to their granddaughter Susan Daingerfield, who married Senator John Strode Barbour of Virginia. Subsequent owners were Mrs. Barbour's sister, Ellen Daingerfield, and Senator Porter H. Dale of Vermont who directed much alteration and refurbishment of both the house and garden. The National Woman's Party purchased the property from Mrs. Oliver H. P. Belmont in 1929, and named it after her.

Beautifully restored today, the three-story-and-basement house in Federal style is of handmade brick laid in Flemish bond. A mansard roof, dormers, and wide windows with white trim, a double staircase at the entrance, and a walled garden at the side are features that make the exterior distinctive. Inside, the floors are of wide, hand-hewn boards, and the tall paneled doors are fitted with fine old silver hinges and locks (installed by Senator Dale) . A desk once owned by Andrew Jackson and another by Susan B. Anthony are among unusual furnishings in this house, which by a special Act of Congress has been preserved as an historic mansion.

The Octagon

Acclaimed as one of the finest dwellings in the country and another triumph of designer William Thornton, The Octagon (now popularly known as Octagon House) was built by John Tayloe of Mount Airy and completed in 1800. Since 1900, it has been the national headquarters of the American Institute of Architects, and under provision of the Historic Sites Act of 1935 it was designated a National Historic Landmark.

Its background glitters with famous names. Tayloe, a wealthy Virginia planter, was planning a mansion in Philadelphia when George Washington persuaded him that the new Federal city would be a preferable locale.

As the building proceeded Washington was very much interested. A contemporary account observed: "The General frequently watched progress of the work, from his horse, when he visited the embryo city." But he did not live to see it completed.

Tayloe and his wife, a daughter of Governor Benjamin Ogle of Maryland, moved to The Octagon in 1807 and at once began entertaining with extravagant elegance. Their calendar subsided considerably, however, on the outbreak of the War of 1812. A Federalist, Tayloe was completely out of sympathy with the war, but being a patriot, he accepted the post of Cavalry Commander of the District of Columbia. Meanwhile, he removed his family to Mount Airy, and invited Comte Jeane Pierre Serurier, the French Minister, to occupy The Octagon for its protection.

Rear view of The Octagon.

After the White House went up in flames, he turned The Octagon over to President and Mrs. Madison and it served as the Executive Mansion for a year. With delightful Dolley Madison as hostess, the house reached its apex of glamour and power; and it was there that the Treaty of Ghent, officially ending the war, was signed on February 17, 1815. Still standing in the center of the round room, which was Madison's study and is now called the Treaty Room, is the table on which the document was signed.

When the Madisons moved to the Pennsylvania Avenue dwelling that the British Minister, Sir Augustus John Foster, had occupied before the war, the Tayloes returned to The Octagon and resumed their resplendent way of life. After John Tayloe died in 1823, his wife spent much of her time there for the next thirty-two years. At the end of the Civil War, the government took over the house for use as a military hospital. Then it accommodated a girls' school, and later became a temporary government office building. Several Negro families were living in it when the American Institute of Architects took a five-year lease on it in 1897. The institute bought it in 1900, and shortly thereafter initiated a complete restoration program; Stanford White was among the architects active in implementing it.

The house is unique. Ingeniously adapted to the angular site, the English brick structure is not an octagon but rather an elongated hexagon, with a three-story bay and a portico on the front. A flight of steps with lacy handrails and newel-post lamps are at the entrance, and wrought-iron balconies set off the windows of the second floor. The replacement of the original flat deck roof and attic parapet with a hipped roof in 1930 was the only major change from the original design.

Generally known today as Octagon House, the structure has been open to the public for some years. In the latter part of 1968, however, it was closed for extensive renovation. When it is again opened, its classic archways, spiral staircase, and circular vestibule will be among the faithfully restored features that will re-create the aura of its distinguished past, when it was acclaimed the finest house in the Federal City. Meanwhile, its history is recalled less frequently than the ghostly legends that surround the place.

One is about Colonel Tayloe's daughter who, heartbroken when her father refused to consent to her marriage to a young Englishman, committed suicide by flinging herself over the great staircase. The story goes that her shade wanders nightly on the premises. Another legend has to do with a murdered slave whose spirit explores secret underground passages from The Octagon to the Potomac and the White House each evening, although both tunnels were walled up long ago. The ghost of the ill-fated Aaron Burr, who made a final call on Dolley Madison at The Octagon before he left in disgrace for England, is another reported to haunt the house.

Meridian House

From the standpoint of both taste and magnificence, the mansion at 1630 Crescent Place is perhaps the finest house ever built in Washington. Of limestone and reinforced concrete, it is a notable example of the Louis XV style, inside and out, and its grace and grandeur imply that it might have been ordered for a titled European centuries ago.

Actually, it was designed by John Russell Pope and built in 1922 for Irwin Laughlin, who had been Ambassador to Spain and Minister to Greece. Today it is Meridian House, owned by the Meridian House Foundation and providing offices for the Washington International Center, the Foreign Student Service Council, the Institute of International Education, the Institute of Contemporary Arts, and The Hospitality and Information Service for Diplomatic Residents and Their Families (THIS). With a charming terrace and a garden to the rear, the house is on an acre and a half of ground in a quiet area off Sixteenth Street.

Containing forty-five rooms on four floors, the palatial structure is equipped with an elevator, and is richly furnished. Two massive front doors open into the ground floor, which originally was given over to servants' quarters but now is a large reception room. A sweeping double staircase reaches to the second, or main, floor. The parquet floor in the drawing room is covered with oriental rugs in dulled tones of red, rose, blue, and cream. Dove-gray walls, their gesso embellishments defined by gold leaf; Louis XV sofas and chairs upholstered in gold satin; and exquisite Chinese screens and vases are also located in this elegant salon.

What was once the formal dining room is now an assembly hall, but still the dominant focus of interest in it is the handsome Mortlake tapestry from the Netherlands, a prize possession of the late Irwin Laughlin.

An especially charming area is the oval loggia, which has white Moroccan rugs on its highly polished marble floors, Louis XV chairs, and marquetry tables. *Torchères* match the period and scale of the room. The walls are a soft gray. On either side of the doorway to the entrance hall are stone sphinxes. French doors from both the drawing room and the loggia give access to the garden, enclosed by a stone wall and shaded by linden trees.

Irwin Laughlin died in the 1930's, and, after Mrs. Laughlin's death early in 1958, their daughter Mrs. Hubert Chanler put the house on the market. Under a grant from the Ford Foundation, it was bought in 1960 to serve as an International Center, perhaps in the hope that the Latin motto carved over the massive oak door leading to the foyer might hold true. It reads: *Quo habitat felicitas nil intret mali* ("Where happiness dwells, evil shall not enter").

The graceful double staircase of Meridian House, leading to the loggia.

The lounge to the left of the loggia.

Anderson House, from
Massachusetts Avenue.

The great hall, with the
portrait of Mr. and
Mrs. Larz Anderson
on the balcony.

Anderson House

The nation's oldest patriotic order, the Society of the Cincinnati, has its
national headquarters in Anderson House, at 2118 Massachusetts Avenue.
Another stately mansion, this was built in 1905 for Larz Anderson, onetime
Minister to Belgium and then Ambassador to Japan. A striking example of
the unrestrained magnificence of great turn-of-the-century houses, it was
designed by Little and Brown of Boston and constructed of gray stone.
Seventeen types of marble grace the interior.

The ballroom (thirty by eighty feet) has a balcony approached by a
regal staircase and defined with a wrought-iron railing, a coffered ceiling
thirty feet high, and Louis XV furnishings. An enormous portrait by Philip
Laszlo de Lombos of Ambassador and Mrs. Anderson as they appeared in
1928 is on the balcony wall.

Paintings, letters, medals, and other Revolutionary relics are displayed
on the first floor. On the paneled walls of the library are portraits of the first
two presidents of the society—George Washington, by Gilbert Stuart, and
Alexander Hamilton, by Charles Willson Peale.

193

194

The second floor, with its Brussels tapestries, paintings by Raeburn and Reynolds, and handsome antique furniture is maintained by the Andersons as it was originally. Particularly noteworthy in the dining room, where the floor is of inlaid Italian marble, are the seventeenth-century Brussels tapestries and the Imari bowls that were given to Larz Anderson by the Emperor of Japan. Carved Regency furniture covered with Aubusson tapestry and greige walls picked out with gold leaf accent the French salon, while the gallery, which is eighty feet long, features three Brussels tapestries, along with Italian religious paintings and oriental brocades.

Larz Anderson was himself a member of the Society of the Cincinnati, which was founded by officers of the Revolutionary Army and chartered on May 10, 1783. His widow gave the house and the furnishings to the organization in the 1930's.

The Cosmos Club

Across the street from Anderson House is the Cosmos Club, the Capital residence of Sumner Welles during his term as Undersecretary of State in the Franklin D. Roosevelt administration.

The stately edifice located at 2121 Massachusetts Avenue was designed by the famous New York architectural firm of Carrère and Hastings for Mrs. Richard Townsend, a leader in turn-of-the-century Washington society. Granddaughter of an Erie, Pennsylvania, railroad magnate and daughter of Representative William Scott of Pennsylvania, she was said to be one of the richest women in America; and it was not surprising that she built one of the finest houses in Washington.

She and her husband purchased the site from Mr. and Mrs. Curtis Hillyer. As the story goes, Mrs. Townsend, aware of the superstition that one who moves into a new home after the age of fifty will live no more than a year, ordered incorporated into her house some of the walls from a residence which had been built on the property in 1873, so that the mansion would not be an entirely new one.

The four-story house, dating to 1899, is suggestive of an eighteenth-century château, and reputedly was modeled after the Petit Trianon at Versailles. Patently in the French Renaissance style and of Indiana limestone on a Milford granite base, the mansion has huge double front doors with ornate iron grillwork. The original design included forty-four rooms, which were barely ample for Mr. and Mrs. Townsend, their daughter Mathilde, and thirty-four servants.

The entrance of the Cosmos Club.

195

196

The Warren Lounge of the club was the ballroom in Mrs. Townsend's time.

The massive appearance of the house with its mansard roof, dormers, and four chimneys on the four-story central section is accentuated by wings. Many effects of the original interior are still there. The Louis XVI lobby has walls of Caen stone, columns and pilasters of Breche Violette marble, and a floor of white marble with green Campan borders. The grand stairway, paneled in oak above the first story, has an elaborate wrought-iron railing.

On the second floor are several notable salons. The Louis XV sitting room has an Italian Creamo mantel with bronze appliqué. The Louis XVI sitting room gives prominence to an Italian white marble mantel with pale blue Brocadelli trim and fluted shafts with bronze arrow appliqué. Paneled in French walnut, the library boasts a great fireplace with an overmantel of Devon stone.

The elevator opens on the oak-paneled, Louis XVI–style gallery, which houses a mantel of broad-veined Campan Rubane Mélange with bronze appliqué. The paneled Louis XIV dining room has mantels of Languedoc marble and two consoles.

At the east end of the long gallery is a marble-floored room that was Mrs. Townsend's conservatory. At the west end is the magnificent Louis XIV ballroom, where mirrored walls are embellished by garlands and cupids picked out in gilt, and a white and gold domed and paneled ceiling surrounds a painting of Aurora, goddess of dawn, in her chariot.

In the latter room, Mathilde Townsend made her debut in 1909; and it was there, also, that she was married the following year to her first husband, Senator Peter Goelet Gerry of Rhode Island. President and Mrs. Taft and the entire Cabinet were among the guests.

Acknowledged grande dame of the Capital, Mrs. Townsend maintained her social supremacy for several years. Invitations to her mansion were as eagerly sought as were those to the White House. An Austro-Hungarian minister who had general reservations about American society is reputed to have said that "to dine at Mrs. Townsend's off bouillabaisse, washed down with Chateau Yquem, and pheasant with rare, sparkling burgundy would be compensation for a post in the heart of Africa."

Her house had been planned to take care of two or three exclusive dinners a week, and sizable receptions and supper parties twice a month during the social season. There was continual activity in the enormous kitchen around a stove with eight coal burners, a broiler, and two fireless cookers; and supplementing one big serving pantry was another with a balustraded balcony bearing shelves for enough house china to supply a buffet for up to a thousand guests.

On Mrs. Townsend's death, the mansion was inherited by her daughter, who by that time was married to her second husband, Sumner Welles. The latter offered the house as a temporary residence for the President-elect and Mrs. Franklin Roosevelt shortly before the inauguration in 1933.

Up until World War II, the dwelling served as the town house for Undersecretary of State and Mrs. Welles, but they preferred their estate at Oxon Hill, Maryland, and spent very little time at the Massachusetts Avenue address. In 1943, the mansion was occupied by more than a hundred

members of the Canadian Women's Army Corps stationed in wartime Washington, while the stable on the grounds served as headquarters for the American Women's Voluntary Services.

After Mrs. Welles died in Switzerland in 1949, the Cosmos Club purchased the mansion from her estate. In August, 1952, after having been ensconced in the Dolley Madison House on Lafayette Square for seventy-four years, this organization moved into its new home.

Under the direction of Horace W. Peaslee, the club did considerable remodeling, and added a wing to the rear to provide more bedrooms and another dining room. Today, there is a front entrance for ladies opening into the ladies' lounge. The coach house on Florida Avenue is an auditorium. What was once the white and gold ballroom is now a lounge, and other areas of the mansion have been rearranged to accommodate the needs of a club. But in general, an air of splendor prevails, as in the days when Capital society revolved around the great house.

The second-floor drawing room of the Arts Club, furnished in keeping with the Monroe era.

The Arts Club

No other organization has headquarters with a more conspicuous link to history than the Arts Club, at 2017 I Street. Known for many years as the Monroe House, it was occupied by the fifth United States President when he was Secretary of State, and later served for several months as the Executive Mansion. It was also the British Legation for several years, and the scene of many notable gatherings.

The land originally was part of the "Widow's Mite," a large tract deeded by the British Crown to Anthony Holmead, an Englishman. Some time after the division of lots for the city of Washington, the site was acquired by James McCubbin Lingan, who had served in the Maryland line during the Revolutionary War. Timothy Caldwell bought the property in 1802 and built a house there, fronting K Street. Three years later, he purchased more frontage from Lingan to erect "the handsomest house in the Capital City." The original structure enlarged and the main entrance changed to I Street, he completed the dwelling in 1806.

For the times, it was a grand house, indeed. In the late Georgian style of red brick laid in Flemish bond and trimmed with white stone, it had three stories and twenty nicely proportioned rooms. Except for later additions of attic dormers, the basic architectural details have remained unaltered since 1806. The Arts Club insignia is a reproduction of the finely arched entrance

Opening into the drawing room, the original sitting room is now a library. The portrait over the mantel is of Henry K. Bush-Brown, noted sculptor and first president of the Arts Club.

with its molded architrave and keystone. The paneled doorway has narrow sidelights and a delicately framed fan transom.

Despite the requirements of a club, the interior is an impressive reminder of nineteenth-century elegance. On the ground floor, to the right of the entrance, the spacious original reception room has three recessed windows on one side, and, on the other, a wide doorway defined by columns that separate it from the dining room. (Both rooms are now the dining area of the club.) A large drawing room, with recessed windows overlooking I Street, opens into the library. Bedrooms occupy the upper floors. Two of the exquisite eighteenth-century chandeliers acquired by the club from an old Baltimore mansion were destroyed in a fire that swept through the house some time ago, but they have been faithfully reproduced in the drawing room as it is today. The plank floors, mantels, and archways were in the original house, and among the other especially interesting features of the interior are the bas-relief garlands on the walls and the mahogany handrail and graceful balusters of the old staircase.

Nothing is more fascinating about this landmark, however, than its history. Caldwell sold the house in 1808 to Postmaster-General Gideon Granger, purchased it back in 1813, and until 1840 retained possession, leasing the place to a number of distinguished tenants. Secretary of State James Monroe was known to have occupied it before the British invasion in 1814.

Monroe and his elegant wife, the former Elizabeth Kortwright of New York, had spent much time abroad while he was twice Minister to France, and had acquired many choice furnishings. Their I Street house, therefore, soon became noted as the epitome of taste and luxury. Mrs. Benjamin W. Crowninshield, wife of the Secretary of the Navy, wrote in December, 1815, of attending a dinner there. Obviously impressed, she dilated on the silver, dishes, and forks—"so heavy I could hardly lift them to my mouth." She described the drawing room as "handsomely lighted—transparent lamps I call them; three windows, crimson damask curtains, tables, chairs and all the Furniture French; and the andirons, something entirely new." After Monroe was inaugurated on March 4, 1817, the house became the Executive Mansion and remained so until September, when the President and his family moved into the renovated White House.

The next noted tenant of I Street was the British Minister Stratford Canning, who moved the British Legation there from 2618–2620 K Street. The handsome thirty-five-year-old bachelor was reputed to have been so avidly pursued by Washington widows and debutantes that he finally and firmly declined to pay court to any of them singly in their homes. But he invited them, en masse, to his numerous receptions where members of his staff could protect him. One of the most brilliant social affairs under his aegis, however, had a romantic angle—the marriage of his attaché, William Gore Ouseley, and Marcia Van Ness, niece and adopted daughter of General and Mrs. John Peter Van Ness. Three hundred notables attended the civil marriage, performed in the Legation under British law and the British flag, following the religious service at St. John's Church.

Canning's successor, Charles Richard Vaughan, resided in the I Street house during his first term as minister. Another popular bachelor, the fifty-year-old envoy furnished the place with handsome English effects and boosted his popularity and Britain's prestige with a steady series of brilliant social events. Josiah Quincy, who had served as representative from Massachusetts and was Mayor of Boston in 1826, was among guests at a gala ball given by Minister Vaughan that year. Quincy later wrote that it was the finest of all functions he had attended. Dancing was held in the large upstairs drawing room, and midnight supper was served on the ground floor.

Vaughan also made headlines as host to some celebrated British visitors, among them Mrs. Anthony Trollope and Harriet Martineau; but the significant achievement of his career was the firm friendship he established with President Andrew Jackson during the hectic "Peggy O'Neill Eaton" affair. While several foreign envoys, following the example of Vice President and Mrs. John C. Calhoun, ostracized the questionable beauty who was the wife of Jackson's Secretary of War, Vaughan gave a big ball and paid her the honor of the evening by escorting her in to supper. "Old Hickory" never forgot.

Successive occupants of the house after Vaughan were the Austro-Hungarian Minister, the Baron de Mareschal, Charles Francis Adams, and General Silas Casey. Francis Markoe, Jr., who was in the State Department and was also president of the Columbian Institute, purchased the house in 1849, and leased it briefly to Virgil Maxcy, former Solicitor of the Treasury. In 1877, Markoe sold the property to Cleveland Abbe, head of the United States Weather Bureau. Abbe made several minor changes and additions to the dwelling, but took great care not to destroy its architectural character. After Abbe died in 1916, the house for a brief time became the St. John's School for Girls; but in May of that year it was purchased by the Arts Club.

The International Eastern Star Temple

The wedge-shaped mansion at 1618 New Hampshire Avenue, where the Prince of Wales stayed for ten days during his visit to Washington in 1919, was called by the unkindly "the opening wedge," when it was built by Perry Belmont in 1909.

His wife, the former Jessie Sloan, had divorced her first husband to marry Belmont, and straight-laced society lifted its collective lorgnette at the pair who, presumably, expected the mansion to be their opening wedge to

The library.

The International
Eastern Star Temple,
1618 New Hampshire
Avenue, was once the
home of Perry
Belmont.

204

exclusive acceptability. If that was the purpose, it worked out successfully, for in time the house drew not only Washington notables but those from all over the world.

The eldest son of August Belmont, New York representative of the House of Rothschild, who later became Minister to the Netherlands, Perry Belmont had served in Congress from 1881 to 1889, and had also been Minister to Spain when he decided to build his opulent house in the Capital city. He employed as architect E. Sanson, of Paris, under the direction of Horace Trumbauer, who later designed the Philadelphia Art Museum. The result is a triangular limestone mansion with fifty-four rooms occupying an entire block.

In the Louis XIV manner, the finely conceived exterior has ornamental arches, pedimented windows, an urn-crowned balustrade around the eaves, a shaded porte cochere, and splendid wrought-iron and glass entrance doors. There are three stories above the basement, and the latter alone was designed with eleven rooms, two baths, and a squash court.

The mansion now is the International Temple of the Order of the Eastern Star; but among its appointments are many that distinguished the house at the time of the lavish entertaining of the Belmonts.

Chandeliers throughout are of gold and bronze with imported, hand-carved rock crystal drops, some interspersed with amethyst. The parquet floors and woodwork are of quarter-sawed oak. Door fixtures are of bronze. The eleven mantels were brought from European palaces. Walls of the lobby are of Caen stone, and sconces are covered with ten-carat gold.

A Japanese hand-embroidered, four-fold teakwood screen faced with a royal hunting scene, a gift from the Emperor of Japan to Mr. Belmont, highlights the treasure room on the second floor. Over the mantel hang ruby and porcelain girandoles with rock crystal drops. A fine fruitwood table, a Moorish chair, and an intricately carved Italian chair are in this salon as well.

The dining room.

A hand-carved table, an elaborate china cabinet, and thirty chairs with cut-velvet cushions are in the dining room, which is a reproduction of a room in the Doges' Palace, Venice. Teakwood tables, Chinese blue and gold draperies, an ornate brass incense burner, Chinese porcelain and tapestries give the Chinese room its name; while the ballroom, paneled in gilt, with gold brocade draperies and mirrors and murals, is the acme of elegance in the tradition of a European court. An extraordinary piece in it is a French table with a large "Portrait of Verona" in the center and twelve portraits around, all on ivory.

The Belmonts went abroad in the late 1920's, and put the house on the market. Probably because of the Depression, there were no buyers; and in 1933 Belmont got authorization to convert the mansion into an apartment house. But the project never went into effect. The Order of the Eastern Star purchased the property in 1935, to serve as its national headquarters and International Temple.

SELECTED BIBLIOGRAPHY

ADAMS, HENRY. *Life of Albert Gallatin*. Philadelphia: J. B. Lippincott Co., 1902.

ADAMS, JOHN QUINCY. *The Lives of James Madison and James Monroe*. Boston: Phillips, Sampson & Co., 1850.

ANDERSON, ISABEL W. *Presidents and Pies*. Boston: Houghton Mifflin Company, 1920.

BALCH, THOMAS BLOOMER. *Reminiscences of Georgetown, D.C.* Washington, D.C.: Henry Polkinhorn, 1859.

BEALE, MARIE. *Decatur House and Its Inhabitants*. Washington, D.C.: National Trust for Historic Preservation, 1954.

BRIGGS, EMILY EDSON. *The Olivia Letters*. Washington, D.C.: Neale Publishing Company, 1906.

BROWN, GLENN. *Memories; A Winning Crusade to Revive George Washington's Vision of a Capital City*. Washington, D.C.: W. F. Roberts Co., 1930.

CARPENTER, FRANK G. *Carp's Washington*. New York: McGraw-Hill, 1960.

COLBY, NATHALIE SEDGEWISK. *Remembering*. Boston: Little, Brown and Company, 1938.

COLMAN, EDNA M. *Seventy-five Years of White House Gossip, from Washington to Lincoln*. New York: Doubleday, Page & Co., 1926.

COMSTOCK, HELEN. *The 100 Most Beautiful Rooms in America*. New York and London: Thomas Y. Crowell in association with Studio Publications, Inc., 1958.

DAVIS, DEERING, DORSEY, STEPHEN P., and HALL, RALPH COLE. *Georgetown Houses of the Federal Period*. New York: Architectural Book Publishing Co., 1959.

Decatur House. Washington, D.C.: National Trust for Historic Presentation, 1967.

EBERLEIN, HAROLD DONALDSON, and HUBBARD, CORTLAND VAN DYKE. *Historic Houses of Georgetown and Washington City*. Richmond, Va.: Dietz Press, 1958.

ECKER, GRACE DUNLOP. *A Portrait of Old George Town*. Richmond Va.: Garret & Massie, 1933.

ELLET, E. F. *Court Circles of the Republic*. Hartford, Conn.: Hartford Publishing Co., 1870.

EVANS, HENRY RIDGELY. *Old Georgetown on the Potomac*. Sold by the Georgetown *News*, 1933.

FALES, WINIFRED. "The Lindens, A House with a History," *Antiques* magazine (February, 1938).

FINLEY, DAVID E. *History of the National Trust for Historic Preservation, 1947–1963*. Washington, D.C.: The National Trust, 1965.

GORDON, WILLIAM A. "Old Homes on Georgetown Heights." Paper read before the Columbia Historial Society, March 17, 1914.

GREEN, CONSTANCE MCLAUGHLIN. *Washington, Village and Capital, 1800–1878*. Princeton, N.J.: Princeton University Press, 1962.

HELM, EDITH BENHAM. *The Captains and the Kings*. New York: G. P. Putnam's Sons, 1954.

HURD, CHARLES. *Washington Calvacade*. New York: E. P. Dutton & Co., 1948.

JACKSON, RICHARD P. *The Chronicles of Georgetown, D.C. from 1751–1878*. Washington, D.C.: Henry Polkinhorn, 1878.

JACOBSEN, HUGH NEWELL. *A Guide to the Architecture of Washington*. New York: Frederick A. Praeger, Inc., 1926.

KEYES, FRANCES PARKINSON. *Capital Kaleidoscope*. New York: Harper & Brothers, 1937.

LEARY, JOSEPHINE DAVIS. *Backward Glances at Georgetown*. Richmond, Va.: Dietz Press, 1947.

LEECH, MARGARET. *Reveille in Washington*. New York: Harper & Brothers, 1959.

LOCKWOOD, MARY SMITH. *Historic Homes of Washington*. Washington, D.C.: D. C. Belford Co., 1889.

LONGWORTH, ALICE ROOSEVELT. *Crowded Hours*. New York: Charles Scribner's Sons, 1933.

MACKALL, SALLY SOMERVELL. *Early Days in Washington*. Washington, D.C.: Privately printed, 1899.

MCLEAN, EVALYN WALSH (with BOYDEN SPARKS). *Father Struck It Rich*. Boston: Little, Brown and Company, 1936.

MARTINEAU, HARRIET. *Society in America*. London: Saunders & Otley, 1837.

MOORE, CHARLES. *Washington Past and Present*. New York: The Century Company, 1929.

MORGAN, GEORGE. *The Life of James Monroe*. Boston: Small, Maynard & Company, 1921.

MORRISON, HUGH. *Early American Architecture*. New York: Oxford University Press, 1952.

NEVINS, ALLAN (ed.). *The Diary of John Quincy Adams (1794–1845)*. New York: Charles Scribner's Sons, 1951.

NICOLAY, HELEN. *Our Capital on the Potomac*. New York: The Century Company, 1924.

PALMER, JOHN WILLIAMSON. "Old Georgetown—A Social Panorama," *Century Magazine* (April, 1897).

PINCI, A. R. "The New Washington," *Munsey's Magazine* (August, 1915).

POLLOCK, QUEENA. *Peggy Eaton, Democracy's Mistress*. New York: Minton, Balch & Company, 1931.

QUINCY, JOSIAH. *Figures of the Past*. Boston: Roberts Brothers, 1883.

SLAYDEN, ELLEN MAURY. *Washington Wife (1897–1919)*. New York: Harper & Row, 1962.

SMITH, MARGARET BAYARD. *The First Forty Years of Washington Society*. New York: Frederick Ungar Publishing Co., 1906.

TAGGART, HUGH T. "Old Georgetown." Paper read before the Columbia Historical Society, May 13, 1907.

THORNTON, MRS. WILLIAM A. "The Diary of Mrs. William A. Thornton," entries from the year 1800, Columbia Historical Society Records, Vol. X.

TORBERT, ALICE COYLE. *Doorways and Dormers of Old Georgetown*. Georgetown, D.C., 1932.

TOWNSEND, GEORGE ALFRED ("GARTH"). *Washington Outside and In*. Hartford, Conn.: J. Betts & Company, 1873.

TUCKER, GLENN. *Poltroons and Patriots*. New York and Indianapolis: The Bobbs-Merrill Co., 1951.

WARDEN, DAVID BAILLE. *A Chorographical and Statistical Description of the District of Columbia, the Seat of the General Government of the United States*. Paris: Smith & Co., 1816.

Washington, City and Capital. American Guide Series. Washington, D.C.: Government Printing Office, 1931.

WATERMAN, THOMAS TILESTON. *The Dwellings of Colonial America*. Chapel Hill, N.C.: University of North Carolina Press, 1950.

WECTER, DIXON. *The Saga of American Society*. New York: Charles Scribner's Sons, 1937.

WHITEHILL, WALTER MUIR. *Dumbarton Oaks, the History of a Georgetown House and Garden, 1800–1966*. New Haven, Conn.: Belknap Press of Harvard, 1967.

WILLIAMS, GEORGE LIVINGSTON. *The Gardens of Hillwood*. Washington, D.C.: Privately printed by the Corporate Press, 1965.

WILLIAMS, HENRY LIONEL and OTTALIE K. *Great Houses in America*. New York: G. P. Putnam's Sons, 1966.

WILSON, EDITH BOLLING. *My Memoirs*. New York and Indianapolis: The Bobbs-Merrill Co., 1939.

DESIGNED BY SALLY STEIN
COMPOSED BY AMERICAN BOOK-STRATFORD PRESS, INC.
IN LINOTYPE BASKERVILLE WITH DISPLAY LINES IN MICHELANGELO TITLING
PRINTED BY THE GARRISON CORPORATION
COLOR SEPARATIONS BY SMEETS WEERT, THE NETHERLANDS
BOUND BY AMERICAN BOOK-STRATFORD PRESS, INC.